# THE FOUR LOVES

## & THE LATTER-DAY SAINTS

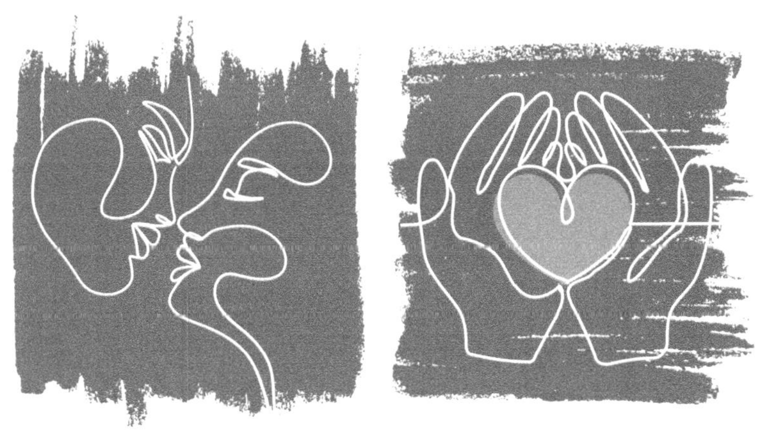

THE NATURE OF LOVE
IN ALL FACETS OF OUR LIVES

# THE FOUR LOVES

## & THE LATTER-DAY SAINTS

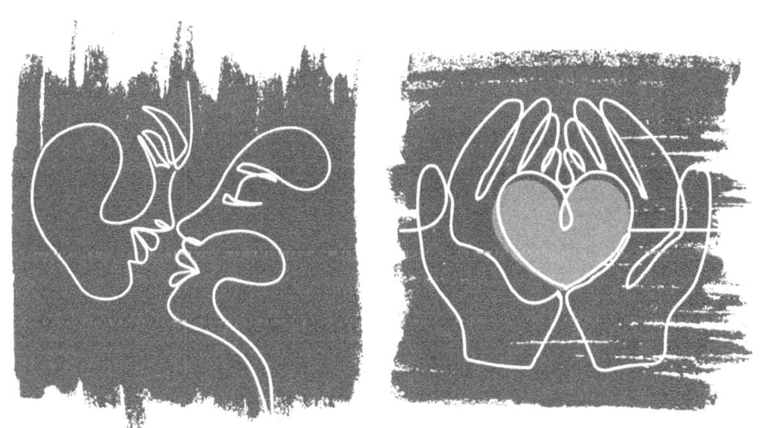

THE NATURE OF LOVE
IN ALL FACETS OF OUR LIVES

BY CASEY PAUL GRIFFITHS
Illustrations by MCKENZIE WISE

CFI
An imprint of Cedar Fort, Inc.
Springville, Utah

ISBN 13: 978-1-4621-4442-6

Published by CFI, an imprint of Cedar Fort, Inc.
2373 W. 700 S., Suite 100, Springville, UT 84663
Distributed by Cedar Fort, Inc., www.cedarfort.com

Library of Congress Control Number: 2023934986

Cover design by Shawnda Craig

Typeset by Kyle Lund

Printed in the United States of America

10 9 8 7 6 5 4 3 2 1

Printed on acid-free paper

*For Elizabeth, as they all are.*

# Other Books by Casey Paul Griffiths

*What you Don't Know About the 100 Most Important Events in Church History*

*Truth Seeker: The Life of Joseph F. Merrill, Scientist, Educator, and Apostle*

*50 Relics of the Restoration*

*50 More Relics of the Restoration*

*Search, Ponder, and Pray: New England Church History Guide*

*Search, Ponder, and Pray: Historic Kirtland Church History Guide*

*Search, Ponder, and Pray: Missouri Church History Travel Guide*

*Search, Ponder, and Pray: Illinois Church History Travel Guide*

# CONTENTS

# Acknowledgments

This project is the child of many parents. Its origins stretch all the way back to the early years of my university studies, when I became enamored with the writings and life of C.S. Lewis. I have enthusiastically read everything he has written that I could get my hands on. When my oldest child left home I gave her a book full of devotionals from C.S. Lewis, and I can pay no higher compliment than that to any author.

As I matured my greatest teacher with regards to the sacred nature of love became my wife, Elizabeth. We have been married for over two decades now but it feels like a blink. It also gets better every day. My relationship with her has defined my understanding of each of the four loves. I don't think I could have written this book before she came into my life.

My children in turn, introduced new kinds of love and affection into my life. Each of them came into this world with a totally unique personality. The gifts they brought with them and their capacity to love teaches me something new every day of my life.

In addition to having a beautiful wife and a wonderful family, I am also fortunate to have a large professional family at Brigham Young University. My fellow teachers in Religious Education have also played a key role in shaping my thought and my teaching with regards to the nature of love. There are too many names to list here but the first that come to mind are

Mike Goodman, Mark Ogletree, Barbara Morgan Gardner, Justin Dyer, Ty Mansfield, and Jenet Erickson. In addition to them I have had literally thousands of influential voices influence this book, specifically the students in my classes at BYU. Love is a subject that everyone has had experience with, and I have benefited immensely from the wisdom and insight shared by my students.

Finally, I wish to express my gratitude to Angela Johnson, who encouraged me to move forward and even expand my thoughts on this subject. Valerie Loveless and Dru Huffaker also provided invaluable help in coordinating my efforts with Cedar Fort. Editing and suggestions for this book were also provided by the tremendous staff of the Faculty Publishing Service at BYU. Heather Randall led the team during the writing of this book, and Kim Sandoval was the primary editor who helped shape and refine this book.

Finally my thanks to all the people of the Harvest Hills 9th ward and in The Church of Jesus Christ of Latter-day Saints, who helped me draw closer to the true source of love for every woman and man. My sincere hope is that the experiences I have shared can help us all know what love is and how to love more deeply.

# Introduction: What Is Love?

*"I love you."*

No phrase is filled with more anxiety, vulnerability, or longing as those three words. We speak them to those we care most about, hopefully with great frequency. Our songs, poems, and popular entertainment are inundated with the consciousness that love is the greatest and most desirable word. Film characters breathlessly say phrases like, "Love is like oxygen! Love lifts us up where we belong—all you need is love!" The word is used so much in our popular discourse that it almost loses meaning and grows beyond examination. We are so in love with the idea of love that we don't often think carefully about what it really means.

In the English language, "I love you" means different things in different contexts and with different people. When an engaged couple says "I love you" it means something very different than when a mother or father says "I love you" to a child. Platonic friends of the same gender might in a hesitant way admit, "I love you, man," embarrassingly and half-seriously expressing the closeness they feel with a person they have no romantic interest in. The gospel of Jesus Christ, with its embrace of the needy and the stranger, even allows us to say "I love you" to a complete stranger with all sincerity. In each case, "I love you" takes on a completely different meaning. In some languages, there are different words to denote familial, friendly, charitable, and romantic forms of love. But in English there is only one phrase, "I love you," that is used with our relative, friend, lover, and even a stranger.

Sometimes this limitation in our language can lead to confusion. Growing up I was infatuated with a beautiful young lady whose family was also close to my family. For years I pined after her romantically, especially because we connected as such good friends. We laughed, confided with each other, and shared our hearts in the way two people can when they have similar interests and see the beauty in each other's souls. I spent most of my teenage years longing to be more than friends. At this point in this kind of story, the narrator usually says that he or she longed for a romantic connection but worried about losing the friendship. I wasn't worried about that—I was more afraid of rejection. Though we spent hours in conversation, making each other laugh and sharing our feelings, she never gave any indication of a desire for anything more than a friendship, so I withheld any attempts to move the relationship in a romantic direction. Still, I loved the way she treated people, and I loved to hear her laugh. That sustained me, though a romance seemed unlikely.

I grew up and left town, then received a mission call and prepared to leave home, following the traditional rite of passage for young men of our faith. Before I left, our families went on one last vacation to Disneyland together. I saw my missionary service as a new phase of my life, but I still longed for connection with her. One day, fate intervened. As we stood in one of the long lines at the amusement park, talking and laughing, a ride operator asked for two riders. I grabbed her hand and we ran on the ride, leaving our families behind with a number of people ahead of them. We rode the ride, and then we ran through the park together the rest of the day without our families. She had a magical way of making everything around her exciting and joyful. We pretended to be an engaged couple, talked with other families in line about our upcoming wedding, and generally just engaged in the kind of goofball adventures only close friends generally can. We had so much fun the first day that we found an excuse to leave the larger group together each day after. I remember watching fireworks with her close to me and wondering if I had really found love in the magic kingdom.

We returned from the trip with only about a week and half until I reported for my missionary service. The approaching deadline heightened the intensity of our relationship as we went to dinner and movies, walked, talked, and spent every night together. Finally, the last night of my adolescent life arrived. I knew if she had romantic feelings for me, she would finally say it tonight. It was now or never.

To ensure maximum closeness, I picked her up on my old 1968 Honda motorcycle, and we drove into the desert. We talked as the rickety motorcycle creaked its way up and down the sagebrush hills surrounding our town. Finally, we stopped and walked through the hills as the sun went down and the world around us grew crisp and cool. We looked up at the stars and talked about our lives, hopes, and dreams. I waited for her to finally say how she felt, to tell me at last that we were more than friends. We spoke as two close people can, but I failed to discern if she saw me as her dear friend, or something more. With the hour getting late, I dejectedly started the motorcycle and left behind the pristine skies of the desert. I drove her back to her car, gave her a long hug, and then said, "I guess I'll see you again in two years."

She looked at me and said, "I love you." Because she was the kind of person who said those words to a lot of people, including her friends, I saw no promise in the phrase. "I love you too," I said, and then turned to get on my motorcycle. As I walked away, she reached out, grabbed my arm, spun me around, and said, "No, I really love you." At that moment I should have burst into song, swept her into my arms, and kissed her. The music would swell, the credits would roll, and we would walk into a perfect sunset, holding hands and gazing at one another with everlasting adoration. Jane Austen, were she still living, would surely contact us for the story rights and memorialize this as one of the great love stories of all time.

What happened instead has haunted me ever since.

Instead of responding like any normal human would, I shrugged my shoulders, looked slightly confused, and said, "Okay, well, see ya." I hopped on my motorcycle, started it, and drove away. It was two blocks later when I skidded to a stop in the middle of the road and half mumbled the words "I love you." You see, dear reader, I thought she was saying "I love you," when what she was really meant was "I love you." I spun around as fast as possible, driving recklessly at top speed to our rendezvous point. There was still time!

There wasn't. She was gone and her car was gone. I could still see the dust she made when she pulled out, and I went to her house, hoping to catch her. Her car was not there. I drove to every place of significance in our friendship. She was nowhere to be found. Apparently, she was so devastated by my brusque reply that she drove around the rest of the night trying to cope with her feelings. I searched for her the next day but failed to find her. At 6 p.m. I was officially set apart as a full-time missionary, and I left town for two years the day after.

We wrote to each other, but I never found the courage to ask directly about what she meant that night. We filled our letters with the kind of banalities people write when they are dancing around what they really want to say to each other. When I returned home, we did finally date, even walking in the desert a few more times, and I am happy to say that that special young lady is now . . . my friend on social media.

I don't spend a lot of time dwelling on this episode. We are both married and have families, and if the incident of that night ever comes up between us it is more likely to generate laughter than heartache. But what caused us to miss our moment? Language, pure and simple.

Had I been a little older, wiser, or just more perceptive, I might have known what her "I love you" really meant. Body language, tone of voice, or just the simple fact that she said "I really love you" might have cued me in to the real meaning of her words. But language has always been an awkward way to communicate. Her words had to cut through a cloud of my own insecurities, foibles, and downright dunderheadedness. A beautiful moment was shattered by my lack of perception. Knowing a little more about love might have made a big difference at the time.

Love is complicated; but understanding it, or at least attempting to, is vital to our joy in this life. Joseph Smith taught, "If men do not comprehend the character of God they do not comprehend themselves." One of the simplest expressions of God's character is Jesus's declaration that "He that loveth not knoweth not God; for God is love" (1 John 4:8). The word appears dozens of times in the scriptures, often meaning different things. The scriptures are full of varied kinds of love stories. The Book of Genesis talks about Jacob serving seven years to win the hand of Rachel, noting that his labors "seemed unto him but a few days, for the love he had" (Genesis 29:20). This situation is completely different than when David learns of the death of his friend Jonathan and laments, "Thy love to me was wonderful, passing the love of women" (1 Samuel 1:26). These two loves, both sacred, are wholly different from the description that "King Solomon loved many strange women" (1 Kings 11:1).

When I went to college, I discovered the works of C. S. Lewis, including a small, short book entitled *The Four Loves.* The book is relatively short but contains a few insights that have been helpful to me over the years as I married, became a father, and started a career of teaching and counseling young people. In the book, Lewis points out that in Greek, the original language of the New Testament, there are four different words for love, each with a different meaning. The four loves are

- *Philia*: friendship love or brotherly/sisterly love
- *Eros*: romantic love
- *Storge*: familial love or affection
- *Agape*: Christlike love or charity

I am no Greek scholar, but at times understanding the differences in these loves greatly enlightens our understanding of the text. For instance, in John 21 an exchange between Simon Peter and the resurrected Christ is recorded as follows:

> So when they had dined, Jesus saith to Simon Peter, Simon, son of Jonas, lovest thou me more than these? He saith unto him, Yea, Lord; thou knowest that I love thee. He saith unto him, Feed my lambs.
>
> He saith to him again the second time, Simon, son of Jonas, lovest thou me? He saith unto him, Yea, Lord; thou knowest that I love thee. He saith unto him, Feed my sheep.
>
> He saith unto him the third time, Simon, son of Jonas, lovest thou me? Peter was grieved because he said unto him the third time, Lovest thou me? And he said unto him, Lord, thou knowest all things; thou knowest that I love thee. Jesus saith unto him, Feed my sheep. (John 21:15–17)

In the King James text, it looks like the Savior is playing verbal games with Peter, repeating back the passage even after Peter provides a clear answer. In the original Greek, however, the exchange is much different. The Savior asks, "Simon, son of Jonas, Agape me?" Simon, responds, "Yea, Lord, thou knowest I Philia thee." The exact interpretation of the text is difficult to discern, but some scholars believe Jesus was asking if Peter loved Him in a pure, exalted, Christlike way. Peter was responding that he loved Jesus as a brother or a friend. The second time the Savior asks, "Simon, son on Jonas, Agape me?" A second time Peter responds, "Yea, Lord, thou knowest I Philia thee." The third time, the Savior changes His approach and asks, "Philia thou me?" Peter responds, "Lord, thou knowest all things; thou knowest that I Philia thee," to which the Savior responds, "Feed my sheep."

It is possible Peter was responding out of insecurity because of the events surrounding the Savior's death, or out of humility because he did not feel he was on the same level as the Savior. The Savior invited Peter to engage in a higher type of love—*agape*, or charity—but was also willing to meet Peter where he was. Peter later adds charity to the list of virtues associated with the partakers of the divine nature, right after brotherly kindness (1 Peter 1:7). Mastery of a lesser love often leads to mastery of a higher love.

The model C. S. Lewis created with these four distinctions is immensely useful in understanding not only the scriptures but also the relationships in our lives. As a young man I devoured the book, highlighting meaningful passages in the text, especially those linked to Eros. I recently reread the text and found a number of different insights, finding myself drawn to the text's discussion on all the loves. Before I had dreamed only of romantic love, not realizing the holistic joy found in experiencing all of the loves God plants in the hearts of His children.

I also found certain limitations in the way Lewis wrote his book. He adds insights from the text of the Bible, his extensive knowledge of literature, and his own experiences. The Restoration of the gospel in the latter days brought forth new texts, ancient and modern, that enlighten our understanding of the nature of God and therefore the nature of love. Each of the four loves was not only discussed by prophets and apostles in ancient times, but also by their modern counterparts. The doctrines and principles revealed through the instruments of His latter-day prophets, under the direction of Jesus Christ, add key insights into the nature of love, particularly its nature outside of the realm of mortality. In the revelations about the premortal realm we see love coalesce in our hearts when we receive a new beginning as spirit sons and daughters created by Heavenly Parents. In the revelations explaining our life in the postmortal realms of eternity, we see love growing to not only fill our worlds but also to create new worlds. In the doctrine of the restored gospel, every time a couple kneels over the sacred altars of the temple, a new universe in embryo is formed and watered by the loves shared by those who are sealed together with the promise of eternity.

Well-meaning Latter-day Saints often speak excitedly of becoming like God and gaining the cosmic powers to bring worlds in and out of creation. This is a part of God's work, no doubt, but it is secondary to the labors of our Heavenly Parents to "bring to pass the immortality and eternal life of man" (Moses 1:39). Before we can master the infinite expanse of the universe, we must master the intimate nature of human hearts. If God is love, then to become like God we must master love by learning the potential of love in all its forms and manifestations. Those who think seriously about the nature of God must begin to realize that the most important lessons of our mortal experience consist of our first efforts to master Eros, Philia, Storge, and most of all Agape, or Charity, the pure love of Christ (Moroni 7:47).

# Prelude: The First Love Story

Imagine Adam and Eve walking slowly as they cross the threshold of Eden and enter the world of mortality. Did they hold hands, seeking warmth as they entered into a world of cold? Did they look at each other with love and affection, knowing that at least they could have each other as they walked into an uncertain future? Did they feel overwhelmed and anxious about the world they traveled toward? They likely felt a mixture of all these things. The primal story of the human race allows us to project our own hopes and fears onto our first parents because what we experience today is not very different from what they experienced back then. They are us, and we them, as we walk with uncertainty into a world teeming with danger and possibility.

Some religious traditions associate the Fall of Adam and Eve with forbidden love, choosing each other over a righteous devotion to God. This does not align with the text in ancient and modern revelation. God not only creates Adam and Eve in the image of the divine, but He also commands them to "be fruitful, and multiply, and replenish the earth" (Moses 2:27–28). The command not to eat the fruit of the tree knowledge of good and evil comes next. President Dallin H. Oaks teaches that the Father's commandment to multiply and replenish was "first in sequence and first in importance. It was essential that God's spirit children have mortal birth and an opportunity to progress toward eternal life."[1]

The Book of Mormon adds invaluable insight to the story of the Fall. The Prophet Lehi, most likely quoting from the brass plates, adds invaluable clarity to our understanding of the environment our first parents entered into. In most Abrahamic religions, the Garden of Eden is viewed as a paradise—making Adam and Eve, ungrateful, naive, and sinful to ever take any action leading to their expulsion. In a discourse given on his deathbed, Lehi paints a much more complex view of Eden. "Behold, if Adam had not transgressed he would not have fallen, but he would have remained in the garden of Eden," Lehi teaches. "And all things which were created must have remained in the same state in which they were after they were created; and they must have remained forever, and had no end." Then Lehi adds the most important nuance to the tale, "And they would have had no children; wherefore they would have remained in a state of innocence, having no joy, for they knew no misery; doing no good, for they knew no sin" (2 Nephi 2:22–23). Not only did Adam and Eve lack the power to live both commandments in their primal state, but they also had to make a choice between them to learn good from evil, keeping with Lehi's earlier teaching that in order for agency to exist there must be opposition (2 Nephi 2:11). Adam and Eve were meant to be one flesh, but before the Fall, did they love each other?

The text suggests that the introduction of sin into the world was not the only consequence of the choice made in Eden. Love was also introduced. How could Adam and Eve know love if they knew no joy, or misery, no good, or sin? Isn't love the most joyful and good thing in our lives? If these things did not exist, then love did not exist. When Eve ate the fruit and left her state of innocence, did she realize for the first time that she loved Adam? When Adam ate the fruit, did he see Eve with the eyes of love for the first time? Did Satan, attempting to create misery among God's children, also set free our greatest joy? The scriptures teach that Satan "knew not the mind of God, wherefore he sought to destroy the world" (Moses 4:6). Latter-day revelation confirms that the Fall was a fortunate one, bringing death and sorrow but

1 "The Great Plan of Happiness," *Ensign*, November 1993.

also the love of genuine relationships with all their bittersweet ecstasy. "Adam fell, that men might be, and men are that they might have joy" (2 Nephi 2:25).

The revelations of the Restoration ask us to reimagine the departure of Adam and Eve from Eden as an event not only of dread and fear, but also of hope and attachment. They chose each over a paradisiacal state. In his fictionalized rewrite of the Fall, Mark Twain added that Adam realized that Eden was "wherever Eve was."

In the moment of the Fall, Eros and philia must have overwhelmed the first couple. Adam and Eve realized their attraction for each other and their sense of relief over having a companion with them in a world of uncertainty. Storge was next born out of their love and friendship. The tender language of scripture records, "And Adam knew his wife, and she bare unto him sons and daughters, and they began to multiply and to replenish the earth" (Moses 5:2). They moved from couplehood to family life as sons and daughters joined them in mortality.

There was one more type of love necessary for them to fully comprehend mortality. The restored text of Genesis adds this episode:

> And after many days an angel of the Lord appeared unto Adam, saying: Why dost thou offer sacrifices unto the Lord? And Adam said unto him: I know not, save the Lord commanded me.
>
> And then the angel spake, saying: This thing is a similitude of the sacrifice of the Only Begotten of the Father, which is full of grace and truth.
>
> Wherefore, thou shalt do all that thou doest in the name of the Son, and thou shalt repent and call upon God in the name of the Son forevermore. (Moses 5:6–8)

The last part of their love story was in place. There was a way for their feelings to continue on in the eternities, and love could transcend the travails of their mortal life. Agape, or charity, was explained to them fully through its purest expression, the sacrifice of Jesus Christ. Hearing this, Adam rejoiced, declaring, "Blessed be the name of God, for because of my transgression my eyes are opened, and in this life I shall have joy, and again in the flesh I shall see God" (Moses 5:10). Eve was a touch more perceptive, adding inclusive pronouns as she expressed her joy: "Were it not for our transgression we never should have had seed, and never should have known good and evil, and the joy of our redemption, and the eternal life which God giveth unto all the obedient" (Moses 5:11). Knowing about the highest form of love purified and cleansed the impurities of all the types of love they felt.

Adam and Eve's experience with the angel is currently missing from the biblical narrative and was restored by the Prophet Joseph Smith. For most Christians the signature story of this phase of their love story is the death of Abel at the hand of his brother Cain, undoubtedly a piercing introduction into the vulnerability of loving and being loved. Losing a child is difficult under any circumstances, but such a violent act rends the hearts of all involved. The hidden part of the story is that even while Adam and Eve buried their child, they knew he was not lost forever. A plan was in place to return what they lost through the "merits, mercy, and grace of the Holy Messiah" (2 Nephi 2:8).

Adam and Eve still held onto each other, but now they fully knew the meaning of loss and death in the world they lived in. Shaken with the loss of a child, would their love for each other stay strong? And would their children find love and joy, or sorrow and loss in the new and complicated world they chose over the Garden of Eden?

# Eros

*"There is not a more pure and holy principle in existence than the affection which glows in the bosom of a virtuous man for his companion."* —Parley P. Pratt

What Is Eros?

Eros, or romantic love, is the most well-known of the four loves. In our current culture it is almost impossible to escape. It is celebrated in poetry, music, cinema, and nearly every kind of form of art known to humanity. Nearly any person can rattle off different phrases in their head that directly correspond to the feeling of being in love. "Love is like oxygen—Love lifts us up where we belong—All you need is love!" Eros—or being in love—is one of the great obsessions of our current culture. Songs and poetry talk about the exhilarating feeling of meeting someone new, realizing mutual attraction, and then experiencing the feelings of closeness that come from realizing someone loves us too. We cry and cheer when on-screen couples connect and kiss, and then the screen fades to black. Why are we so obsessed with Eros? *Because it is so great.*

While our discussions about Eros in Church settings often revolve around chastity and its importance, we sometimes forget that our theology is strongly in favor of Eros. "Consider the power of the idea that of all people on earth, we Latter-day Saints know the most about genuine romantic love," taught Elder Marlin K. Jensen.[2] Romantic love is the foundation of not just our theology, but also our perception of the universe. "Our theology begins with heavenly parents," taught President Dallin H. Oaks, "Our highest aspiration is to be like them."[3] Consider for a moment the power of that idea. We believe that everything in the universe, all the surrounds us, all that makes us happy and gives meaning and purpose to our existence, is the result of a loving union between a Celestial Father and a Celestial Mother. They love each other romantically, and out of that love the universe was born, including the sons and daughters of this union of love. Not only did their love and attraction, their Eros, lead to the creation of mankind, but they intended for their children to experience Eros as well. The first and most important commandment given to Adam and Eve in the Garden of Eden was, "Be fruitful, multiply, and replenish the earth" (Moses 2:28).

Not only was this commandment one of the first teachings found in the scriptures, but it has also been re-emphasized in the last days. Joseph Smith and all the prophets of the Restoration have taught that Eros between a man and a woman is a gift from God that is intended to make us happy here on earth and usher us into the eternities. Early Apostle Parley P. Pratt was completely overwhelmed by the eternal nature of Eros when it was taught to him by Joseph Smith. "I received from [Joseph] the first idea of eternal family organization, and the eternal union of the sexes in those inexpressibly endearing relationships which . . . are at the very foundation of everything worthy to be called happiness," Parley wrote after a discussion with Joseph Smith. Having been raised outside of the restored gospel of Jesus Christ, Parley had always assumed that Eros was a fixture of mortality, not something that could blossom as a part of eternal life. "Till then I had learned to esteem kindred affections and sympathies as appertaining solely to this transitory state, as something from which the heart must be entirely weaned, in order to be fitted for its heavenly state," he added. Reflecting years later on this lesson, Parley wrote:

---

2 Marlin K. Jensen, "A Union of Love and Understanding," *Ensign,* October 1994, https://www.churchofjesuschrist.org/study/ensign/1994/10/a-union-of-love-and-understanding?lang=eng

3 Dallin H. Oaks, "Apostasy and Restoration," *Ensign,* May 1995, 84, https://www.churchofjesuschrist.org/study/general-conference/1995/04/apostasy-and-restoration?lang=eng.

> It was Joseph Smith who taught me how to prize the endearing relationships of father and mother, husband and wife; of brother and sister, son and daughter.
>
> It was from him that I learned that the wife of my bosom might be secured to me for time and all eternity; and that the refined sympathies and affections which endeared us to each other emanated from the fountain of divine eternal love. It was from him that I learned that we might cultivate these affections, and grow and increase in the same to all eternity; while the result of our endless union would be an offspring as numerous as the stars of heaven, or the sands of the sea shore. . . .
>
> I had loved before, but I knew not why. But now I loved—with a pureness—an intensity of elevated, exalted feeling, which would lift my soul from the transitory things of this grovelling sphere and expand it as the ocean. I felt that God was my heavenly Father indeed; that Jesus was my brother, and that the wife of my bosom was an immortal, eternal companion; a kind ministering angel, given to me as a comfort, and a crown of glory for ever and ever. In short, I could now love with the spirit and with the understanding also.[4]

Eros is good. Latter-day Saints should not be afraid or ashamed to talk about Eros and the power it has to enrich and enliven our lives. If our highest aspiration is to become like our Heavenly Parents, feeling Eros is among the greatest joys of our life.

## Eros and Sex

C. S. Lewis wisely observed, "Sexual experience can occur without Eros, without being 'in love,' and Eros includes other things besides sexual activity. . . . Sexuality may operate without Eros or as a part of Eros."[5] In our society today, Eros is often thought to be the same thing as sexual attraction, and that misconception is part of the problem. Sexuality is a biological function, and part of experience here on earth, but it is not always associated with Eros. Experiencing Eros with another person often results in an impulse to want to touch, caress, or experience physical intimacy with them.

---

4 Parley P. Pratt, *Autobiography of Parley P. Pratt* (Salt Lake City, UT: Deseret Book, 1979), 297–98.

5 C. S. Lewis, *The Four Love,* (San Diego, CA: Harcourt Brace, 1960), 91–92.

As a young student in a college psychology class, I remember our professor calling up a male and female student as part of a role-play in class discussion. He asked us to imagine that the couple (who didn't know each other, and giggled through the whole experience) were genuinely in love. Then he asked us how we would be able to tell that they were in love from external observations. "They will want to hold hands!" came one reply, which produced a wave of immature laughter from the class. "He will want to kiss her!" brought even more giggles. All of the frivolity in the room was suddenly silenced when the professor bluntly stated, "Will he want to have sex with her?" No one spoke. We were all chuckling before, but now you could have heard a pin drop. The professor looked at us intently, allowing silence to completely fall over the room. Finally, one person in the class said, meekly, "No, he won't want to do that if they love each other." The professor cocked his head to the side, raised an eyebrow, and said, "Really? If they actually, truly, deeply, love each other?" We just sat there in an awkward silence. We were willing to giggle and laugh about holding hands and kissing, but suddenly the discussion had gotten deeply personal; the professor had broached a topic many of us were not ready to discuss.

The truth is that sexuality is a component of Eros. It is okay for us to talk about it and acknowledge it as a part of the experience of being in love. At the same time, sexuality is not wholly synonymous with Eros. Eros is much larger than just the sexual attraction two people feel for each other. Feeling a physical attraction toward another person does not mean that you are in Eros with them. In fact, an overemphasis on sexuality and its relationship to Eros can be damaging and dangerous. Quoting historians Will and Ariel Durant, Elder Jeffrey R. Holland once noted "that sex is a river of fire that must be banked and cooled by a hundred restraints if it is not to consume in chaos both the individual and the group."[6] Because of the inherent dangers surrounding violations of the law of chastity, our approach toward discussing Eros and sexuality has largely centered on preventing people from violating Church standards. This avoidance of sin is good and proper, but only discussing Eros in terms and sexuality and chastity leaves a gap in our knowledge.

Of the four loves, Eros is perhaps the least steady. This might be why is it so often likened to fire in our discussions about it. Fire is undoubted-

6 Jeffrey R. Holland, "Personal Purity," *New Era,* February 2000, https://www.churchofjesuschrist.org/study/new-era/2000/02/personal-purity?lang=eng

ly useful. It is a chemical reaction that provides us with warmth from the cold and light in the darkness. But it can also be dangerous when used unwisely. Two pitfalls can sometimes lead us down the road to discontent and unhappiness. The first is when a couple does nothing to nourish or feed the fire that provides the warmth of companionship and closeness that comes from Eros. The second pitfall is an overemphasis on Eros, which can cause the fire of our emotions and attractions to become destructive and harmful. Like a campfire in a cold wilderness, Eros can be a vital tool for our well-being, or, if left unchecked, a spark that leads to untold destruction.

## Interlude: Two Wrinkled Hands

Abram and Sarai sat on top of a hill, gazing out over the land of their inheritance. They had come to this land a lifetime ago, when Abram was only sixty-two years old and Sarai was fifty-two, just a young married couple by the standards of the Book of Genesis (Abraham 2:14). They arrived in Canaan with practically nothing. Abram wrote poetically that "eternity was our covering and our rock and our salvation" (Abraham 2:16). At the time Canaan was a hostile place and Abram and Sarai "called on the Lord devoutly, because we had already come into the land of this idolatrous nation" (Abraham 2:18). In the years that followed they had experienced losses and gains, and the travails of a nomadic existence. But the one constant was the love they felt for each other.

Now Abram was ninety-nine and Sarai was eighty-nine. They had long passed the stage of their lives where their love was driven by physical attraction. Abram reached over with his wrinkled hand and grasped the wrinkled hand of his wife. Sarai was so striking in her younger years that her beauty literally put Abram's life in danger when he entered into a foreign court. The rulers of other nations desired her because of her loveliness, and only quick thinking and fast talking on Abram's part kept them from slaying him to seize his wife.

Now, in what they thought was the twilight of their lives, the Lord had spoken to Abram again. "My covenant is with thee, and thou shalt be a father of many nations" (Genesis 17:4). The Lord promised to give

Abram and new name - Abraham, meaning a father of many nations. He also promised a new name for Sarai - Sarah, both names meaning "princess" in Hebrew. The Lord added, "I will bless her, and give thee a son also of her: yea, I will bless her, and she shall be a mother of nations" (Genesis 17:16).

Now using their new names Abraham and Sarah contemplated how it was possible to have a child at their ages. They long knew of God's promise to Abraham, and had even employed a surrogate at Sarah's request, Hagar, to fulfill the promise the Lord made to them. They now loved and nourished the child, Ishmael, thinking the Lord's promise was fulfilled in him. But this promise was even more specific. Sarah, even in her advanced age, would be the mother of the child. The two grasped each other's hands even more tightly, wondering how an octogenarian and a man one year away from being a century old could have a child.

A few days later three holy men visited Abraham and Sarah. Abraham welcomed them into his tent, while Sarah prepared food and other hospitalities from these visitors of the Lord. Sarah went into a different room of the tent, eavesdropping on the her husband's conversation with these holy men. In the course of their discussion, these messengers from God repeated the Lord's promise, "Sarah thy wife shall have a son" (Genesis 18:10).

Sarah's response? She laughed. She may have stifled the sounds, but she could not keep a straight face at the ridiculous prospect of her and Abraham, at their ages, having a child. "After I am waxed old shall I have pleasure, my lord being old also?" (Genesis 18:12). Her laughter might not have reached the ears of the men in the other part of the tent, but it did reach the Lord.

The Lord spoke to Abraham, asking him why Sarah laughed at His promise, and short comedic episode ensued as Sarah tried to hide her mirth from an all-seeing, all-knowing being. Sarah dared to continue to laugh, now out loud, telling the Lord, "Shall I of a surety beat a child, which am old?" The Lord assured her, "Is anything too hard for the Lord?" (Genesis 18:13-14).

The three holy men left, and Abraham and Sarah, the mother and father of nations, sat together in their tent. Could they still have a child? Would Sarah be the mother of the covenant people of God? Abraham gazed and Sarah, her face weathered and worn from years of nomadic living in the deserts of Canaan. They had grown only together. In the final years of their lives would they finally see a child born from their love?

Abraham did not know how or when this blessing would come. But one thing was for certain. Sarah was the great love of his life. Whether she bore a child or not, their Eros remained undimmed by the decades of time they passed together. As Sarah reached over and grasped Abraham's hand, she knew that - come what may - he was her intimate partner in all parts of her life. Their love was the beginning of a story that would bless all the nations of the earth.

## Nourishing Eros

When we are young, Eros comes naturally, almost overwhelmingly to us. We seek love constantly and fall into infatuation easily. It is normal and natural for us to do this. The fire of Eros burns brightly and leads most people to choosing a companion. But the unsteady nature of Eros at times makes such a relationship difficult to sustain over long periods of time. Eros, like a fire, must be continuously fed and nurtured. If we assume that the spark of attraction that brought us together will sustain itself forever, we are foolish. We must instead feed the fire and tend to it in order to keep it burning. It is possible for a couple to be married for decades and still experience intense Eros for each other. It is also possible for a couple who only rely on the initial spark and chemistry from when they first met to fall out of love. If their Eros is not tended to and kept burning bright, Eros often grow weak and then exhausts itself.

A few years ago, I served as an ecclesiastical leader in a very young ward. Most of the families in our ward were in their mid-twenties with one or two children. As I met with couples to counsel them, a common theme emerged among the couples who were struggling in their marriages. "I don't know him/her anymore," was the most common way these feelings were expressed in my counseling sessions with these couples. I listened carefully to what both spouses had to say, and I tried to seek the Spirit to know the right words to help these couples heal their unions. Over several months of counseling with young couples, I saw a common pattern. Most of these couples had very young children at home. I would ask a question like, "When was the last time you spent time together—just the two of you?" The answers to this question were strikingly similar. Nearly every couple replied by saying something like, "We haven't really had any time together since the baby was born," or "We have hardly been alone since I started my job," and so forth. Most of the couples felt they were doing fine when I asked about many of the common red flags in troubles marriages, such as communication or finances. When I asked a blunt question like, "Do you still *like* each other?" the answer was also usually a quick "yes."

So what was the problem? Most of these couples had not deliberately or maliciously made an effort to fall out of love. They just stopped being romantic. They stopped nourishing their Eros, usually because their schedules became too full with other responsibilities, and the fire had ebbed and died. They didn't feel like they were in love anymore because they stopped doing the things people do when they fall in love. As just one example, in a situation where parents devote all of their time to a small child, it can be easy to neglect the romantic part of your relationship. The same neglect can also come about if we place too high a priority of work, hobbies, or other things that can draw focus from our loved ones. In a society where we visualize success as something that happens in the workplace and not in the home, it can be easy to neglect a partner's emotional needs. This neglect might manifest as simply as when everyone uses their own screen to watch their own show, and no one shares the experience of watching something together.

Instead of associating the word "sex" with Eros, I wish we would associate the word "intimacy." As Lewis points out, Eros and sex are not synonyms. Eros is much more than just sex. Likewise, intimacy is much more than just physical intimacy. In recent years, family therapists have begun to shift the use of the term "intimacy" away from meaning just physical intimacy and have started to point out other ways that couples can be intimate with each other. Consider the following types of intimacy:

- Emotional intimacy: being on the same wavelength and feeling close.
- Intellectual intimacy: sharing thoughts and ideas.
- Aesthetic intimacy: sharing the beauties of the world.
- Creative intimacy: sharing acts of creating together.
- Recreational intimacy: playing together, having fun.
- Work intimacy: sharing common tasks in closeness.
- Conflict intimacy: facing and struggling with challenges and differences.
- Crisis intimacy: coping together with problems and pain.

- Spiritual intimacy: experiencing the uniting of spirits, sharing spiritual experiences.[7]

When we only think of intimacy as a synonym for sex, we can miss out on a lot of wonderful experiences, and it may also limit our opportunities to experience physical intimacy. But each of these different kinds of intimacy require effort to cultivate.

The kinds of intimacy you experience may very depending upon the interests of you and your partner. If both of you enjoy the kind of exhilaration that comes from the energy of a crowd at a sporting event, you can experience this intimacy which a stadium full of your closest friends. If you appreciate nature and the beauty of the world around you go one a hike, visit a national or state park, or just arrange an outdoor adventure. If you or your partner enjoys being creative, take an art class, or maybe even try instruction in social dance.

When we think of intimacy only in terms of physical intimacy, we greatly limit the way we can share ourselves and experience intimacy. In turn, if a couple isn't experiencing any of these other kinds of intimacy, it is likely that they will not feel close to each other; and if they don't feel close to each other, they probably won't experience physical intimacy either. The fire of Eros grows cold, and we feel that we are no longer "in love."

In a similar fashion, a couple doesn't have to experience physical intimacy to be close to each other. I know a couple where one partner encountered serious health issues that limited the physical part of their relationship. They are still one of the most intimate couples I know. They talk all day together, share meals, make plans, and are hardly ever even in a different room. One of the most intimate experiences of my life occurred when my wife and I found out that a couple we were close with were separating and contemplating a divorce. We stayed up late talking about what we could do to help the couple, how to avoid some of the problems they faced, and how grateful we were to have each other. There was no physicality involved, just long and meaningful conversation with each other. We experienced crisis intimacy as we worked to resolve this difficult and traumatic problem. When the Lord told Adam and Eve that "by the sweat of thy face thou shalt eat bread" (Moses 4:25) it was both a curse and a blessing. Their labor, their suffering, and their sorrows were a way to create togetherness.

---

7 I am indebted to Ty Mansfield for sharing his research with me on these different types of intimacy.

For the couples I counseled, their feeling of not being love usually came from a lack of conscious effort to nourish their Eros. For most of them, the solution was to recognize the problem and create time to be alone and experience romance. This could take the form of a regular date night, a stroll in the evenings after the events of the day had quieted down, or just sitting on the couch and watching a program together. Here are a few suggestions to nourish Eros:

1. Schedule time to talk every day. Set aside your concerns, your responsibilities, and most importantly, your devices, and listen to one another.
2. Find a time to be alone together. This can be difficult with younger children, but it is worth the effort to find a babysitter and have a night out.
3. Schedule an overnight date or trip every two to three months. Go somewhere that allows you to escape from your regular responsibilities and settings.

This won't look the same for every couple. A few years ago, my schedule shifted so that I was teaching class in the evenings, and it became difficult to find a regular night to go on a date. Instead, my wife and I walked our daughter to school together every morning and then came home and made breakfast together. The time we spent together was invaluable. In another example, early on in our marriage, we created a "cooperative" with two other couples who lived nearby. Each week one couple would watch all the children at their home while the other two couples went on dates. This meant that we had ten screaming children in our house every three weeks, but in the end it was a positive experience for our children and us. Efforts like this are the equivalent of carefully monitoring and stoking the fire of Eros so that it doesn't burn out and become cold. This is just as important for older couples as it is for new couples. Without care, Eros can burn itself out and grow cold.

A regular date night can be a great way to create different kinds of intimacy, but sometimes schedules or tight finances won't permit even one night a week to go out together. In these cases intimacy can still be created by finding time to spend alone together, talk together, or experience closeness. One couple I knew just made it a priority to be in the same room together whenever possible. In a world where the number of distractions is rapidly multiplying, just the act of giving someone your attention can be very intimate. But it might require you to put down your device, set aside messages or other distractions, and just genuinely devote your time to the person you love.

### Bridling Eros

In much of today's culture, Eros has become synonymous with love. Eros is love, but we often treat Eros like it is *only* the kind of love. Placing too much emphasis on Eros can be just as dangerous as putting too much fuel on a fire. It is true that God implanted attractions within us, but if we treat these feelings as though they are the only path to satisfaction in life, we miss out on much of the joy God wants to offer us. Especially in its early stages, Eros can become obsessive, making us neglect the other relationships in our lives that our vital to our happiness.

Further, when sexuality is divorced from Eros we end up with blind, wanton lust—something that can truly destroy the relationships we cherish. When a person looks at pornography, for example, they are not experiencing Eros. There is none of the warmth, care, or reciprocation of feelings that comes from truly being love. There is only an object of gratification. Sometimes if we overemphasize the sexual aspect of Eros, we can deeply hurt those who we are truly in love with. The writer of Proverbs warned, "Can a man take fire in his bosom, and his clothes not be burned? Can one go upon hot coals, and his feet not be burned? . . . Whoso committeth adultery . . . destroyeth his own soul. A wound and a dishonor shall he get; and his reproach shall not be wiped away" (Proverbs 6:27–28, 32–33).[8]

It is true that these desires are built into us, are natural, and come from God. But any desire can become damaging to us if overindulged. When discussing this concept in my classes, I usually put a picture of a sugar cookie on the screen. Everyone agrees that cookies are delicious. Then I ask, what if your appetite for cookies became so great that you thought about them all the time? What if you searched the Internet for photos of cookies? What if you sought out nothing more than to view or look at cookies every moment when you were alone? By this point everyone in the room knows we aren't talking about cookies. The adversary seeks to take the natural, good gifts we have been given from God and then seeks to twist and change them into things that hurt us. Alma counseled his son Shiblon to "see that ye bridle all your passions, that ye may be filled with love" (Alma 38:12). Passion is a

8 See Holland, Personal Purity.

great part of life, but left uncontrolled, our physical appetites don't lead us to Eros, only to ruin and bitterness.

Likewise, treating Eros as if it is the only type of love can leave us unfulfilled. I have no doubt that, after our relationship with God and Jesus Christ, our relationship with our spouse is the most important in our life. But to place all of our happiness, contentment, and fulfillment on just that one relationship is too much pressure. The most fulfilled people I know have a network of people they can connect with as a support system to help them find satisfaction and joy. This is largely why a clear understanding of the other loves—Philia, Storge, and Agape—is so important to our development into complete beings.

Just like the songs, poems, and films all say, Eros is one of the greatest things in the world. But it is not the only love we need to learn in this world.

# Interlude: On the Shores of the Mississippi River

Joseph Smith stood on the landing near the Nauvoo House, a Church-owned hotel built by the Saints in their new home on the Mississippi River. He watched with anticipation as the Maid of Iowa, a small steamship, chugged its way slowly upriver. Among the passengers on the Maid of Iowa stood Elder Parley P. Pratt, returning from a three-year-long mission to the British Isles. Parley was one of the earliest converts of the Restoration, and one of Joseph's dearest friends. He was returning home with his wife, Mary Ann, and their five children. The youngest child, a daughter, was only 3 or 4 days old.

A large congregation surrounded Joseph on the landing, and as the ship docked there was a "general handshaking" as long-separated friends and family welcomed each other home to the new settlement of the Latter-day Saints. Joseph, unable to wait any longer, boarded the ship and walked into the cabin where Parley and Mary Ann's family waited to disembark. After greeting his old friend, he sat down and placed two of their children, Parley Jr. and Nathan, upon his knees in an affection gesture. The Prophet was suddenly overcome with emotion. Noticing the change in his friend, Parley remarked, "We took away three children and have brought back five." Joseph, with tears streaming down his face, replied, "Well, well, Brother Parley, you have returned bringing your sheaves with you." Taken aback by the deep feeling manifested by the Prophet, Parley joked, "Why, Brother Smith, if you feel so bad about our coming home, I guess we will have to go back again," and he began to weep his own tears of joy. According to one observer, "This broke the spell—smiles returned, and joy unbounded filled every heart."[9] Joseph later recorded in his official history, "I was present at the landing, and the first on board the steamer, when I met Sister Mary Ann Pratt (who had been to England with bro. Parley) and her little daughter, only 3 or 4 days old." He added, unashamedly, "I could not refrain from shedding tears."[10]

Today the sight of two grown men bursting into the tears upon seeing each other might be an object of derision, or at the very least some teasing. Yet it remains a fact that the kind of love we call friendship can be one of the greatest sources of joy in this life. "Let me be resurrected with the Saints, whether I ascend to heaven, or descend to hell, or go any other place," Joseph Smith declared. "If we go to hell, we will turn the Devils out of doors and make a heaven of it. Where this people are, there is good society. What do we care where we are if the society be good?"[11]

We seek out fellowship like we do water, and to be deprived of it can be just as fatal as the deadliest thirst. "Loneliness is the global epidemic of our time," decries one headline, and the number of studies by social scientists on this plague multiplies. According to one study, a lack of social connections is as damaging to our health as smoking 15 cigarettes a day, and loneliness is potentially twice as bad for older people as obesity, and almost a great a cause of death as poverty.

---

9 Mary Ann Stearns Winter reminiscences, 11, Church History Library, Salt Lake City, UT.

10 "History, 1838–1856, volume D-1 [1 August 1842–1 July 1843]," p. 1529, The Joseph Smith Papers, https://www.josephsmithpapers.org/paper-summary/history-1838-1856-volume-d-1-1-august-1842-1-july-1843/172

11 "History, 1838–1856, volume E-1 [1 July 1843–30 April 1844]," p. 1680, The Joseph Smith Papers, https://www.josephsmithpapers.org/paper-summary/history-1838-1856-volume-e-1-1-july-1843-30-april-1844/50

And this plague is just as prevalent among the young as it is among the poor.[12]

We seek connection with others. We die without it. Why, in a time when we seem to be more connected to more people, in more places around the world than we have ever been, do we see an increasing lack of connection to others? And what is the price we are paying for neglecting Philia, or friendship?

12 Tania de Jong, "Loneliness Is the Global Epidemic of Our Times," May 10, 2016, https://www.huffingtonpost.com.au/tania-de-jong/loneliness-is-the-global-epidemic-of-our-times_a_21544979/

# Philia

*"Friendship is one of the grand fundamental principles of Mormonism."* —Joseph Smith Jr.

In the Old Testament, the Prophet Enoch stands as a singular character. Though he is a frequent subject in apocryphal writings, Enoch is only mentioned in six verses of the book of Genesis. His story concludes with the cryptic note that "Enoch walked with God: and he was not; for God took him" (Genesis 5:24). When Joseph Smith began his inspired translation of the Bible, the story of Enoch expanded from six verses to 137! While these verses add immeasurably to our understanding of the scriptures, perhaps the most valuable insight provided by these revelations is that Enoch was not taken to heaven alone. Instead of a lone prophet standing against the rising tide of wickedness, the inspired translation found in the Pearl of Great Price tells the story of a community that gathered together through righteous principles and stood in opposition to a world of rising violence. "And the Lord called his people Zion," the text declares, "because they were of one heart and one mind, and dwelt in righteousness; and there was no poor among them" (Moses 7:18). Without undercutting the importance of a personal relationship with God, the scriptures are direct in telling us that our love for our fellowman is just as important in our progression.

The first step on the road to loving all men and women is to develop Philia, or friendship.

What is Philia? In Greek the word *Philia* denotes love or affection, especially between equals. It is often translated as brotherly or sisterly love. In *The Four Loves*, C. S. Lewis commented, "To the ancients, Friendship seemed the happiest and most fully human of all loves; the crown of life and the school of virtue." He also added, "The modern world, in comparison, ignores [Philia]. . . . Affection [Storge] and Eros [romantic love] . . . you could feel these tugging at your guts and fluttering in your diaphragm. But in Friendship—in that luminous, tranquil, rational world of relationships freely chosen—you go away from all that. This alone, of all the loves, seemed to raise you to the level of gods or angels."[13]

Philia is like a stream of water, flowing gently past us and bringing life to the landscape surrounding it. Just like water, it smooths and softly washes away the hard edges in our nature, making a deep impression over long periods of time. Part of the power of Philia is that it flows easily within the landscapes of our lives. It's constant flow brings life and But just like water, we cannot survive long without Philia.

Water is a potent analogy for the role Philia plays in our lives. I grew up in a small desert town in the western reaches of Utah. The landscape around me wasn't green and lush, but it held its own charms. It was dotted with sagebrush, a hardy plant that needs very little water to survive, and seems to grow everywhere. The land I grew up in seemed designed to highlight to an observer where water was found. Green patches spring out the desert where there is a even a small flow of water. Tall trees, with bright green colors contrast the more subdued desert hues, as water provides the nourishment for the trees to reach heavenward. Only in those places where adequate water is found can a community really take hold and last. In the cold arid deserts of the Intermountain West where my family made our home, water brought life to the land, and that life invited the settlers to build havens where people found refuge and safety from the harsher elements of the desert.

Like the water that brings life to desert communities, Philia is a necessity, but, like that water, it performs its magic so simply and quietly that it is sometimes not noticed until it is in short supply. Philia is a simpler, more quiet kind of love. It is less likely to be accompanied by strong swings

---

13 C. S. Lewis, *The Quotable C. S. Lewis*, ed. Wayne Martindale and Jerry Root (Wheaton, IL: Tyndale House Publishers, 1989), 234.

of emotion or grand gestures. It rolls along smoothly, quietly, consistently, and perhaps with less maintenance than the other loves. It can be a stunning revelation when a person realizes they are in Eros, but a person rarely realizes when they feel Philia for another person—they just like having them around. There can be times when we need to make a deliberate effort to make friends and reach out. But most of the time our friendships grow organically. When I was a child my friendships were almost all determined by geography. There was a little boy the same age as me that lived across the street. We played in the sandbox, watched cartoons, and went on adventures throughout our small town.

As I grew up, friendships developed among my co-workers and my students. Male friendship can be among the greatest joys of life. A fellow teacher I worked closely with became one of my closest friends. This wasn't because we made any direct effort, it just happened naturally. We carpooled to work together, and enrolled in the same graduate program. Soon we were spending more time with each other than we were with our wives. Our work friendship grew into a relationship where we spent part of our free time together as well. It reached a point where my wife rolled her eyes when my friend showed up at our house, or when I took off on another adventure with him and other teachers from work. We were both young fathers with growing families who loved our wives deeply, but there was a special bond of friendship that really enriched my life. Our carpool eventually grew to five other teachers and as the relationships deepened and the number of inside jokes multiplied exponentially, the simple carpool to and from work became one of the most enjoyable and fulfilling parts of my day. A brotherhood can be one of the most fulfilling things we experience in life.

For women, a sisterhood is perhaps even more important. My wife and I live within a twenty-minute drive of every one of her sisters. All of them are very close, and constantly involved in each other's lives. News travels quickly among the sisterhood. Texts come in at all hours of the night and dozens of times throughout the day. When family gatherings happen, all of the sisters are inevitably found in a circle surrounding their mother, laughing and sharing and listening. I have to confess to feeling some jealousy over the amount of time my wife spends with her sisters. And the texting! Oh, the constant texting at all hours of the day! Technology has allowed my wife and her sisters to carry on a conversation that continues at all hours of the day and night. A new question, comment, or inside joke rolls in at an average of about every ten seconds.

All kidding aside, the support system that exists among the sisterhood has also blessed my life in ways I never imagined. Whenever a crisis in the family happens, the sisterhood jumps into immediate action. When my wife's water broke in the middle of the night, one of the sisters was at our door before we were even in the car on our way to the hospital. When there is a emotional crisis, sickness, or hospitalization, the sisterhood descends.

My wife's sisterhood is not only an asset when things go wrong. There are days when the presence of her sisters lifts her spirits in ways that I just cannot. At regular intervals a day spent with the sisterhood allows her an outlet to release her own stress and worries. They also give her a chance to serve and feel needed. My wife is fortunate to have four sisters to create this support system, but her model isn't the only way to create a sisterhood. Sisterhoods come into being through shared interests, values, or just shared geography. The value in gatherings like exercise groups, book clubs, or work friends can often be more in the sisterhoods created. The families we find are often just as important to us as the family we were given. It is a wonderful thing to be part of a sisterhood.

## Philia and the Holy City

In the writings of the early Saints, one consistent thread is a longing for a genuine sense of belonging and community. We sometimes forget that Joseph Smith's concerns during his own search for the true Church centered more on the way other religions' adherents treated each other than on their contending doctrines. "When the converts began to file off, some to one party, and some to another, it was seen that the seemingly good feelings of both the priests and the converts were more pretended than real; for a scene of great confusion and bad feeling ensued—priest contending against priest, and convert against convert; so that all their good feelings one for another, if they ever had any, were entirely lost in a strife of words and a contest about opinions" (Joseph Smith–History 1:6).[14] Before Joseph was told by the Father and the Son that the teachings of the other churches were incorrect, it was the lack of sincere Philia that turned him away from their fellowship.

---

14 "History, 1838–1856, volume A-1 [23 December 1805–30 August 1834]," p. 2, The Joseph Smith Papers, https://www.josephsmithpapers.org/paper-summary/history-1838-1856-volume-a-1-23-december-1805-30-august-1834/2

The idea of a united society of genuine Philia appealed to other converts as well. When historian Grant Underwood undertook a study of early literature produced by the Latter-day Saints in the early period of the Restoration, he found that the two most quoted passages among the early Saints were Ether 13:4–8 and 3 Nephi 21:1–7.[15] What do these passages share in common? Both speak of a new holy city, a new Zion. As he edited the history of the Jaredites, the Prophet Moroni wrote of "a holy city unto the Lord . . . and that a New Jerusalem should be built up upon this land, unto the remnant of the seed of Joseph" (Ether 13:5–6). Similarly, during his visit to the Nephites, Jesus Christ promised "that I shall gather in, from their long dispersion, my people, O house of Israel, and shall establish again among them my Zion" (3 Nephi 21:1).

After the Book of Mormon was published, the building of the holy city became an obsessive project for the Saints. In July 1831, the Lord revealed the location of the holy city to be on the boundaries of the United States and Native American territories, near the city of Independence, Missouri. He also commanded those whom He had chosen to "be planted in the Land of Zion as speedily as can be with their families" (D&C 57:14).[16] As new converts poured into the Independence area, Joseph Smith and other Church leaders began to lay down practical instructions for how the city would be built up. The Plat of the City of Zion—essentially a blueprint for the settlement—was sent to Church leaders in Missouri early in the summer of 1833, illustrating the grand design of the city and the practical details of its creation. Created as a collaborative effort among the members of the First Presidency—Joseph Smith, Sidney Rigdon, and Frederick G. Williams—the plat is essentially the master plan for the city of God. Written around the edges of the plans are detailed notes about the nature of the city. The city was to be one square mile with a grid system outlining rectangular blocks and lots laid out for homes and gardens.[17] It is easy to imagine neighbors in this design of the city of Zion sharing vegetables from their gardens as they engaged in friendly conversation. The city was to be built to bring people together.

---

15 Grant Underwood, "Book of Mormon Usage in Early LDS Theology," *Dialogue* 17, no. 3 (Autumn 1984): 39.

16 "Revelation, 20 July 1831 [D&C 57]," p. 94, The Joseph Smith Papers, https://www.josephsmithpapers.org/paper-summary/revelation-20-july-1831-dc-57/2

17 Richard Francaviglia, *The New Mapmakers of Zion* (Salt Lake City: University of Utah Press, 2015), 31.

The structure of the city was also designed for collaboration in Church responsibilities. At the heart of the city, two prominent rectangles sat with the numbers 1–24 inside of them. These numbers designated a sacred place at the center of the city where a complex of twenty-four temples was to be built. From looking at the plans, we can see that these temples were intended for a different function than current Latter-day Saint temples are. Rather than concerning themselves primarily with ordinances for the living and the dead, these temples were intended to serve as administrative centers. Divisions of three temples each were assigned to various Church organizations. For instance, temples 10, 11, and 12 were designated as "the house of the Lord for the presidency of the high and most holy priesthood." Other temple trios were identified by titles such as "the house of the Lord for the presidency of the high priesthood after the order of [Aaron]," "the house of the Lord for the teachers in Zion," "the house of the Lord for the Deacons in Zion," and so forth. Today, Latter-day Saints associate temples with sacred ordinances, but these temples were designed to be open places of meeting, where groups of priesthood holders could collaborate. The number and titles of the temples correspond with the structure of the Church as it was then known to Church members.[18] Given the way the city was designed, if similar plans were developed today they likely would also include a temple for the Young Women, a temple for the Relief Society, the Primary, and places of meeting for other vital Church institutions. The important lesson from the project was that the heart of the city would consist of people working together as friends for the glory of God and the exaltation of His children.

The Lord didn't intend for the city to become large and impersonal. Though the city in Independence was supposed to be the central place and the starting point for the kingdom of God on the earth, it was not intended to be the only city built after this pattern. In the explanatory notes, the First Presidency explains, "[when] this square is thus laid off and supplied lay off another in the same way and so fill up the world in these last days and let every man live in the City for this is the City of Zion."[19] The early Saints

18 "Plat of the City of Zion, circa Early June–25 June 1833," p. 2, The Joseph Smith Papers, http://www.josephsmithpapers.org/paper-summary/plat-of-the-city-of-zion-circa-early-june-25-june-1833/2.

19 "Plat of the City of Zion, circa Early June–25 June 1833," p. 1, The Joseph Smith Papers, http://www.josephsmithpapers.org/paper-summary/plat-of-the-city-of-zion-circa-early-june-25-june-1833/1.

held on to this utopian dream of filling the world with celestial cities to serve as places of refuge for the righteous, even after Joseph Smith's death in 1844. The year after the Prophet was martyred, Apostle Parley P. Pratt even wrote a piece of speculative fiction where he imagined the world a hundred years in the future, after the Savior had already returned to earth in triumphal glory. Pratt imagined "digging the foundation of our new Temple in the 124th city of Joseph, near where it is supposed the City of New York once stood."[20] The idea of keeping Zion relatively small and personal is mirrored in the present-day structure of the Church. A ward never consists of more than a few hundred members, nor a stake of more than a few thousand. While gatherings like General Conference often serve as a reminder of the gathering strength of God's kingdom, the Lord intended for the Saints to meet regularly in small groups, where they can know most of the people around them. Instead of a metropolis, the Lord saw a small village as the most effective way to encourage the creation of Latter-day Saints. Philia grows best in small groups.

Persecution in late 1833 forced the Saints to temporarily abandon their project to build the city; but in the midst of their travail, the Lord taught them another critical principle about Zion. Even as persecution raged and it looked as though the Saints would lose the sacred real estate intended for the holy city, the Lord in a revelation told them, "Let Zion rejoice, for this is Zion—THE PURE IN HEART; therefore, let Zion rejoice, while all the wicked shall mourn" (D&C 97:21).[21] The location was important—a revelation given only a few months later declared, "Zion shall not be moved out of her place (D&C 101:17)[22]—but the location wasn't the most important thing about the holy city. After all, a city doesn't really consist of streets, trees, or structures. A city consists of people. There is no Philadelphia, a name that means city of brotherly love, without Philia.

The quest to build Zion remained a concern of geography throughout the rest of Joseph Smith's lifetime and for most of the nineteenth century. Zion was built in Kirtland, Ohio; Far West, Missouri; Nauvoo, Illinois.

---

20 Parley P. Pratt, "One Hundred Years Hence, 1945," in *The Essential Parley P. Pratt* (Salt Lake City, UT: Signature Books, 1990), 142.

21 "Revelation, 2 August 1833–A [D&C 97]," p. 64, The Joseph Smith Papers, https://www.josephsmithpapers.org/paper-summary/revelation-2-august-1833-a-dc-97/4

22 "Revelation Book 1," p. 184, The Joseph Smith Papers, https://www.josephsmithpapers.org/paper-summary/revelation-book-1/172

Those who followed in his footsteps carried his ideas to Winter Quarters, Nebraska; and Salt Lake City, Utah. New converts to the Church from around the world saved their funds to travel to Zion by ship, wagon, handcart, or any means available. This geographic centrism stemmed in part from the necessity of building temples. In a discourse recorded in June 1843 by Wilford Woodruff, the Prophet Joseph Smith taught, "what was the object of gathering the Jews together or the people of God in any age of the world[?] The main object was to build unto the Lord an house whereby he could reveal unto his people the ordinances of his house and glories of his kingdom & teach the people the ways of salvation for [there] are certain ordinances & principles that when they are taught and practiced, must be done in a place or house built for that purpose this was purposed in the mind of God before the world was."[23]

In our day, dozens of temples stand in diverse locations around the globe, but has the spirit of gathering—the Philia felt by the early Saints—gone away? In a March 1831 revelation, the Lord gave his expectations for the city, stating "It shall be called the New Jerusalem, a land of peace, a city of refuge, a place of safety for the saints of the Most High God" (D&C 45:66). It was not only to be a place for the Saints, the Lord also declared that "every man that will not take his sword against his neighbor must needs flee unto Zion for safety. And there shall be gathered unto it out of every nation under heaven" (D&C 45:68–69). While the Lord was urging the Saints to exclude themselves from Babylon, he wanted them to include as many of their fellow brothers and sisters as possible. The city of Zion was intended as a refuge for *all* people.

## Philia, Zion, and the Latter-days

The surprising way that Zion developed is that instead of developing the center place first and then the outer stakes, it appears that in the last days the outer stakes will come first, then the center place. Instead of a grand city with a complex of twenty-four temples at its heart, smaller outposts of Zion with a single temple at their heart have sprung up around the globe in diverse locations. While I fully believe that the city of Zion will still be built in Independence, Missouri, hundreds of tiny Zions formed as faithful

23 "Discourse, 11 June 1843–A, as Reported by Wilford Woodruff," p. 43, The Joseph Smith Papers, https://www.josephsmithpapers.org/paper-summary/discourse-11-june-1843-a-as-reported-by-wilford-woodruff/2

Latter-day Saints built communities of friendship in their own countries. In the last few decades a remarkable increase in the number of temples allowed these communities to put temple covenants in the center of their lives.

In my travels the value of these little Zion's becomes apparent. A few years ago I traveled halfway across the globe to visit and research the Latter-day Saint schools in Tonga. At the time I was new to international travel, and a little nervous about going to a country that I knew very little about. I made a few calls ahead to arrange for housing, but other than that I went in very unprepared. My anxiety was peaking when I landed on the main island of Tongatapu.

I soon found that even though English is officially the national language of Tonga, not everyone spoke it, and even when they did, we still had trouble communicating. When I picked up my rental car at the airport I asked the attendant helping me if the car if it had a GPS. He looked at me like I came from another planet. So I repeated the question. He looked even more confused. This is the part where future me needs to interject and explain that by "GPS" I meant a Global Positioning System, or just a map program to help me find my way around the island. What I didn't know is that in Tonga "GPS" is a common abbreviation for a "Government Primary School" or an elementary school. So I thought I was making a pretty reasonable request for a navigation tool, and my Tonga friend thought I was asking if the car had an elementary school inside. Yet we both spoke the same language. After a few moments of confusion he figured out what I was asking for, laughed loudly, and then said, "No, we don't have those."

When I asked how I could find my way to Liahona High School, where I was staying, he simply said, "Just follow the road, it's not a big island." So I set off on the road, and followed it for forty-five minutes until the road literally went into the ocean. I stopped several people for help and they just told me that there weren't really addresses in Tonga, just follow the road. I did this for several more hours, wondering if I would have to sleep on the beach. Finally, a helpful gentleman on the side of the road told me I was close to Liahona High. His precise directions were "go down the road, turn right when you see a palm tree that forks into a Y, then go about a mile and you'll see a big golden angel on top of building." This time the advice paid off. The golden angel was on top of the Nuku'alofa Tonga Temple, and Liahona High School was right next door.

What happened next really touched me. Across the street from the temple there is same very simple housing for temple patrons. There were dozens of people in the courtyard talking, playing games, and cooking food. They saw me get out of my car and immediately rushed over. I felt a wave of relief wash over me as I realized I had a brothers and sisters now to help. The crowd was a group of Latter-day Saints from Ha'api, one of the island groups that make up the kingdom of Tonga. They saw I needed help and immediately sprang into action. In forty-five minutes I had a home to stay in, more meal invitations than I could manage in my eleven days on the island, and my own personal driver, who was literally named Peni Tonga. The rest of the time I was in Tonga I was never alone, my brothers and sisters there made sure that my every need was met. The little community surrounding that temple became a brotherhood and sisterhood that I will always cherish. When a person feels like a stranger, finding your fellow citizens among the Saints was a deeply moving experience (Ephesians 2:19).

## Why Do We Need Philia?

While being lost on an island is a nerve-wracking experience, many of us live on figurative islands of our own design. Few people would argue against the importance of friendship in our lives, but Philia has generally received less attention than Eros. A general trend of life in the 21st century is the decline of social institutions in our lives. There are fewer places where people of different kinds come together to socialize and build friendships. One researcher has noted the decline of bowling leagues as a sign of disconnection in civic life. Bowling leagues, it appears, are only the beginning. Similar declines in the members of civic and charitable organization are becoming evident as well. Where past generations joined softball leagues, book clubs, and so forth, fewer people today are part of any kind of larger organization. The shift appears to be generational. Robert Putnam, the primary researcher behind the study, notes, "It wasn't so much that old members dropped out - at least not any more rapidly than age and the accidents of life had always meant. But community organization were no longer continuously revitalized, as they had been in the past, by freshets of new members. Organization leaders were flummoxed."[24]

While this may seem like just a generational oddity, there are real dangers to the decline of community and connection among us. I teach college students, and among younger people there are urgent concerns about

24 Robert D. Putnam, *Bowling Along: The Collapse and Revival of American Community*, (New York: Simon and Schuster, 2000), 16.

a rising epidemic of loneliness and isolation. In a recent study of nearly 48,000 college students, 64% said they had felt "very lonely" in the previous 12 months, while only 19% reported they never felt lonely, according to the American College Health Association. Students also reported feeling "overwhelming anxiety" (62%) or "very sad" (69%), and that "things were hopeless" (53%). Nearly 12% seriously considered suicide.[25] According to another survey, a record-high 12% of students reported "frequently" feeling depressed during the past year, while 14% said there was a "very good chance" they would seek counseling in college. Nearly 35% of students frequently felt anxious.[26]

Some of these statistics come from better awareness of and testing for mental illnesses. Thankfully, the awareness of mental health is on the rise, and some of the stigma and shame surrounding mental illness has begun to dissipate, though we still have a long way to go. In one of the most touching conference talks I have listened to, Elder Jeffrey R. Holland openly admitted to his own struggles with depression, and he spoke comforting advice to people with mental illness. "Seek the advice of reputable people with certified training, professional skills, and good values," Elder Holland advised. "Prayerfully and responsibly consider the counsel they give and the solutions they prescribe. If you had appendicitis, God would expect you to seek a priesthood blessing and get the best medical care available. . . . Broken minds can be healed just the way broken bones and broken hearts are healed. While God is at work making those repairs, the rest of us can help by being merciful, nonjudgmental, and kind."[27]

Our mental health also blossoms when we work to cultivate Philia in our lives. Mental health advocates have pointed out that social activities decrease stress levels, help manage depression and anxiety, and just provide

---

25 "Fact Sheet: Loneliness on Campus," *The Foundation for Art and Healing*, accessed June 9, 2020, https://artandhealing.org/campus-loneliness-fact-sheet/?gclid=EAIaIQobChMIuO6Qj-X16QIVUfDACh1mvgOvEAAYASAAEgLbePD_BwE

26 Kevin Egan, Ellen Bara Stolzenberg, Hilary B. Zimmerman, Melissa A. Aragon, Hannah Whang Sayson, and Cecilia Rios-Aguilar, "The American Freshman: National Norms Fall 2016," Cooperative Institutional Research Program at the Higher Education Research Institute at UCLA, accessed June 11, 2020, https://www.heri.ucla.edu/monographs/TheAmericanFreshman2016.pdf

27 Jeffrey R. Holland, "Like a Broken Vessel," *Ensign* or *Liahona*, October 2013, https://www.churchofjesuschrist.org/study/general-conference/2013/10/like-a-broken-vessel?lang=eng

more overall satisfaction in life. A number of studies conducted in several different nations over a period of decades consistently showed that greater involvement in social relationships was a factor in lower mortality. One study showed that the risk of death among men and women with fewer social connections was almost twice as high as those with the most social connections. Have social connections was even linked surprising factors, like heart disease. One study showed the isolated individuals were 2.4 times more likely to develop coronary artery disease than those who socialized on a regular basis.[28]

If the benefits are so apparent, then why is Philia so neglected? As mentioned in the previous interlude, C. S. Lewis noted, "To the Ancients, Friendship seemed the happiest and most fully human of all loves; the crown of life and the school of virtue. The modern world, in comparison, ignores it. . . . It is something quite marginal; not a main course in life's banquet; a diversion; something that fills up the chinks of one's time. How has this come about? The first and most obvious answer is that few value it because few experience it."[29] If Lewis wondered at the decline of Philia in a book written more than a half-century ago, we must ask ourselves: Have the forces that led to the decline of Philial relationships among men and women increased or decreased in the ensuing decades?

It is hard to imagine that a scene like Joseph Smith and Parley P. Pratt bursting into tears upon their reunion wouldn't be met without some snickering or derision today. The idea of rugged individualism, that we can handle all of our problems on our own came to be seen as a virtue. In reality, we need people in our lives who we care about. There is no doubt that our relationship with God comes first, and then our relationship with spouses and family come next, but not far behind should be the friendships that make our lives more meaningful. Another modern trend to enshrine being antisocial as some kind of virtue. This attitude usually arises from fear of the stress and anxiety that comes from meeting new people or being in an awkward social situation. I recognize the challenge of social anxiety - I feel it myself to a certain extent- but we need to overcome our fears. The value of Philia and the way it enriches our lives makes it worth stepping out of our comfort zone every now and then. In the scriptures the value of friend-

28 Debra Umberson and Jennifer Karas Montez, "Social Relationships and Health: A Flashpoint for Health Policy," https://www.ncbi.nlm.nih.gov/pmc/articles/PMC3150158/, accessed November 16, 2022.

29 Lewis, *The Four Loves,* 58.

ship was upheld as one of the great joys of life, along side romantic and familial love.

## Interlude: "My Brother Jonathan"

David and Jonathan were unlikely friends. When David arrived in the royal household, Jonathan was already famous for his bravery and exploits in battle. Accompanied only by his armor-bearer, Jonathan infiltrated a Philistine garrison and the two of them single-handedly defeated twenty Philistine soldiers in combat. When they first met Jonathan was already a war hero of great renown among the Israelites, while David was an unknown youth who had never seen combat before. Jonathan was the son of the first king of United Israel, Saul, while David grew up in a humble family of shepherds.

By all accounts David's came from an ordinary family with no noble blood to distinguish themselves. The Old Testament even goes out of its way to explain that David was the descendant of Ruth, a women from Moab, a county that was traditionally aligned against the Israelites. Jonathan grows up in the royal household, but his father the King was jealous, impulsive, and spiteful. Shortly after the story is told of Jonathan and his armor bearer overcoming an entire Philistine garrison, Saul nearly executed Jonathan for a trivial offense. Following the fight with the Philistines, Saul cursed any person who ate of the food that belonged to the Philistines. Jonathan, not knowing his father's decree, ate some honey that he found. For this, Saul tried to have Jonathan killed, and he would have succeeded if the people had not risen up and expressed their disgust with Saul over his intentions.

It is in this trying circumstance that David and Saul first meet. Knowing their circumstances, including the fact that David was secretly anointed by the Prophet Samuel to take Saul's place as the king of Israel, they seemed destined to be enemies. Yet their are more references about the love between David and Jonathan than nearly any other relationship in the scriptures! The biblical writers declares in moving language that "the soul of Jonathan was knit with the soul of David, and Jonathan loved him as his own soul" (1 Samuel 18:1). The two men made a covenant because Jonathan "loved [David] as his own soul" (1 Samuel 18:3). They grew even closer as David married Jonathan's sister Michal, and the two friends became brothers-in-law.

After David carried out the striking act of slaying Goliath, Jonathan's father grew jealous of David and even sought to slay him. King Saul's homicidal tendencies only strengthened the bond between David and Jonathan. Sensing the growing malice in his father, Jonathan warned David to flee and hide himself before the Saul could murder him. Jonathan then tried to reason with his father to stop him in his mad desire to kill David.

After David fled for his life, he still met secretly with Jonathan to find a peaceful way to resolve the conflict. Jonathan told David, "Whatsoever thy soul desireth, I will even do it for thee" (1 Samuel 20:4). In the face of his father's wrath, the the entire might of the monarchy working to drive a wedge between them, David and Jonathan renewed their covenant of friendship because Jonathan "because [Jonathan] loved [David]: for he loved him as he loved his own soul" (1 Samuel 20:17). As David continued to seek refuge from Saul's wrath, Jonathan continued to meet offer friendship and consolation to David. Jonathan offered solace to David and "strengthened his hand in God" (1 Samuel 23:16).

Shortly after this meeting of David and Jonathan, the strength of their goodness and friendship was tested. By a change circumstance, David came upon Saul, who was sleeping an vulnerable. David was tempted to take his sword and end the life of the king, but he chose otherwise. David instead cut off a part of Saul's robe, and then woke him to show him that he could have taken his life. In this moment, even Saul saw David's goodness, declaring, "Thou art more righteous than I: for thou hast rewarded me good, whereas I have rewarded thee evil" (1 Samuel 24:17). Then Saul made an unusual request of David, pleading, "Swear now therefore unto me by the Lord, that thou wilt not cut off my seed after me" (2 Samuel 24:21).

Why would Saul ask David, a man he saw as his mortal enemy, to protect his family, his seed? It is more than likely that he saw the love David and Jonathan held for each other. Saul must have known that David was a worthy guardian for his sons and daughters. The friendship of David and Jonathan played a vital role in proving David's worthiness as the King of Israel.

Sadly, the friendship of David and Jonathan ended in tragedy. Jonathan was loyal to David, but also to his father. He refused to leave his father's side and both were killed in a terrible battle with the Philistines. When David heard of the deaths of Saul and Jonathan he wept and mourned. But the loss of Jonathan was particularly painful for David. The scriptures record his lamentation, "I am distressed for thee, my brother Jonathan: very pleasant hast thou been unto me: thy love to me was wonderful, passing the love of women" (2 Samuel 1:26).

David's friendship with Jonathan was one of the defining relationships of his life. David even admitted the love he had for Jonathan surpassed the love he felt for the women in his life. While friendship is more humble than romantic love, the role of Philia in shaping our lives and bringing us joy is a treasure we can sometimes take for granted. Like our romantic and family relationships must be valued and nourished.

## Cultivating Philia in Our Lives

How do we develop Philia in our lives? This type of love is difficult and does take some effort. C. S. Lewis noted, "Friendship is—in a sense not at all derogatory to it—the least *natural* of loves; the least instinctive, organic, biological, gregarious, and necessary."[30] It can cause us to stretch to reach out to others and form new friendships, but the benefits outweigh the costs. The happiest people tend to have a support system they can draw on to help them deal with the challenges of life. There have been scores of studies conducted on the question of how many friends make a person happiest. One study conducted with 1700 subjects found that those with five friends or fewer had a 40 percent chance of being happy. Ten was the lowest number at which people were more likely to be happy than unhappy. The study

30 Lewis, 58.

also found that those who expressed the greatest happiness had dozens of friends, with the ideal number landing around 33 friends for women and 49 for men.[31]

How do we build relationships like this? Friendship is not as difficult or unnatural as C. S. Lewis makes it sound. Even the most introverted among us seeks out those with similar interests. Here are three suggestions for developing Philia in your life:

1. Seek out organizations that will provide you with opportunities to serve.
2. Emphasize in-person relationships over online socializing.
3. Become genuinely curious about the people and the world around you.

Let's address each one of these suggestions. First, seek out organizations that will provide you with opportunities to serve. While family and God should be our top priorities in this life, community involvement is a good way to grow as a person and make new friends. Church callings can be a major blessing in this respect. Some of my most unlikely friends came because I accepted a calling and was asked to work with someone in my ward.

A few years ago there was an older man in our ward who was a late-in-life convert to the Church. He grew up in a difficult environment and was lacking in many of the social graces. My first two encounters with him came when he walked across the street to yell at me for using a power sander too late at night and when he took me aside after a sacrament meeting to tell me how ill-behaved our children were (he wasn't wrong). I must admit that when he was assigned as my ministering companion I flinched a little bit. An exhausted looking elders quorum president told me that this brother had already worked his way through several companions because he was so hard to get along with. On our first visit, he offended the family we were visiting by berating their children for being too loud during our lesson! It was difficult, but I stuck with him and kept trying to form a genuine relationship with him. As I came to know more of his backstory, I started to appreciate how extraordinary he was for finding and accepting the gospel of Jesus Christ. Somewhere along the way he became my friend. His acer-

---

31 Fiona Macrae, "Want to be Happy? Have 10 Faithful Friends," *Sunday Telegraph*, October 26, 2008, http://eds.b.ebscohost.com.erl.lib.byu.edu/eds/detail/detail?vid=0&sid=3ca89cee-76ab-4461-85c2-64aa684921d0%40pdc-v-sessmgr05&bdata=JnNpdGU9ZWRzLWxpdmUmc2NvcGU9c2l0ZQ%3d%3d#AN=200810261080514

bic personality eventually led to a divorce from his wife, and he lived alone for the last few years of his life. I dropped by his apartment whenever I could, at times bringing along my family so that he had a sense of belonging. When he passed away a few years later, I wept genuine tears. I still miss my friend. I never would have developed this relationship if I hadn't reluctantly accepted a Church calling.

Church is only one place that you can find great people to build relationships with. Stepping out of your comfort zone to invite neighbors over for dinner or a gathering can be another way to reach out. Community service organizations are a great way to build relationships while doing good in the world. There are plenty of opportunities if you look around. Fund colleagues that you can serve and get to know at work. There are opportunities all around to find Philia. Seek them out.

Second, try to find opportunities to socialize in person. Many have connected the recent spike in loneliness with the rise of social media. Online socializing can be good or bad depending on how it is managed. Overexposure to online media is often linked to higher levels of social anxiety and clinical depression.[32] In my own experience with social media, I have noticed that my online relationships are much shallower and less nourishing than my in-person interactions. Because of my work teaching and traveling, I have thousands of online "friends" but very few that I know as people outside of what I see on my screen. While I value these online connections, I have to be realistic about what they actually represent. Online friendship has brought me new voices from around the world, and I sincerely appreciate that. But online friendship isn't a substitute for genuine human interaction.

In addition, what we see on social media often doesn't present a real picture of what our lives are like. Social media is to actual socializing what reality television is to actual reality. We present a very carefully cultivated and manufactured image of ourselves that often doesn't match the real circumstances of our lives. Many of the people I have counseled express dissatisfaction because their life isn't as exciting as what their friends' lives look like on social media. This is a large part of the reason why President Russell M. Nelson and other Church leaders have counseled us to limit our exposure to

32 Conner Jones, "Effects of Media Use on Mental Health Among Adolescents and Emerging Adults," *Intuition: The BYU Undergraduate Journal in Psychology* 11, no. 1 (2015). https://scholarsarchive.byu.edu/intuition/vol11/iss1/2

social media, urging us to "take a break from the fake."[33] Often our depression and dissatisfaction with our lives comes from us mentally competing with something that doesn't really exist in the first place!

Church President John Taylor once warned against giving superficial teachings to people instead of real truth. He referred to such teachings as "fried froth," the kind of thing you could eat all day and yet finish feeling totally unsatisfied. More recently, Elder Jeffrey R. Holland warned against teachers sharing "spiritual twinkies," or teachings filled with spiritually empty calories.[34] Social media is a kind of "fried froth" or "social twinkie." It can give you the feeling of having an active social life, but it is largely empty and can get you caught up in a destructive competition to gather the most followers, obtain the most likes, or post a picture or story not really reflective of reality, and in the end it is not as nourishing as genuine Philia.

Please don't take this as a blanket condemnation of all forms of social media. There is a lot of joy to be found in online interactions. I have found connection, received encouragement and found new ways to help people because of my online life. But rather than being the main way that we socially interact with others, social media is more a side dish in our human interactions. It can give you the kind of immediate rush that eating a sweet treat can also give, but a steady diet of it isn't very nourishing, and eating too much can just flat our make you emotionally sick.

Real relationships come from our genuine love and concern for other people. Even just simple curiosity about the stories and concerns of others can help us broaden our circle of friends. One of my favorite quotes, often attributed to Ellen Parr, is: "The cure for boredom is curiosity. There is no cure for curiosity." Becoming sincerely interested in others is an obvious way to help others become interested in you. In one of the first self-improvement books, Dale Carnegie wrote, "You can make more friends in two months by becoming interested in other people than you can in two years by trying to get other people interested in you."[35] Self-help guru Ste-

33 "President Nelson Tells Youth to Take a 'Break from Fake,'" *Church News,* June 3, 2018, https://www.churchofjesuschrist.org/church/news/president-nelson-tells-youth-to-take-a-break-from-fake-and-help-gather-israel?lang=eng

34 Jeffrey R. Holland, "A Teacher Come From God," *Ensign*, April 1998, https://www.churchofjesuschrist.org/study/general-conference/1998/04/a-teacher-come-from-god?lang=eng

35 Dale Carnegie, *How to Win Friends and Influence People* (New York: Simon & Schuster, 1981), 56.

phen R. Covey phrased it as "Seek to understand, then to be understood."[36] When we become genuinely curious about the lives and interests of those around us, it isn't difficult to make friends. This is in part because Philia is an outward love. At its best it is directed toward others.

C. S. Lewis noted this unselfish quality of Philia, writing, "friendship arises out of more companionship when two or more of the companions discover that they have in common some insight or interest or even taste which the others do not share and which, till that moment, each believed to be his own unique treasure (or burden)." He continued, "In this kind of love, as Emerson said, *Do you love me?* means *Do you see the same truth?*" Friendships can often come from just finding someone who shares a similar perspective on something that is important to us, but it always comes from looking outward, from seeing others and how we can connect with them. "We picture lovers face to face," Lewis adds, "but Friends side by side; their eyes look ahead."[37]

## The Return of Enoch and the Holy City

Imagine Enoch all those millennia ago ascending into heaven with his city—his family, friends, and community—ascending alongside him. Joseph Smith's inspired translation of the Bible suggests that a similar ascension took place for Melchizedek and his city of Salem. The inspired text notes, "His [Melchizedek's] people wrought righteousness, and *obtained heaven*, and sought for the city of Enoch which God had before taken, separating it from the earth, having reserved it unto the latter-days, or the end of the world" (JST, Genesis 14:34, emphasis added). Enoch and the city of Zion he built reflect an extraordinary, but not a singular, example of the power of love to create a covenant community. Melchizedek and the city of Salem show that the experiment can be replicated. When the final history of the world is truly revealed, who knows how many more cities around the world achieved built enough of a heaven on earth that at last they ascended into the true heaven!

Most encouraging of all, Latter-day revelation tells of the return of Enoch's city to earth. As its inhabitants descend from the heavens, they will in turn be met by another city, built on earth in the same spirit of friend-

36 Stephen R. Covey, *Principle Centered Leadership* (New York: Simon and Shuster, 1990), 45.

37 Lewis, *The Four Loves*, 65–66.

ship and love that brought forth Zion thousands of years ago. The creation of not just one, but thousands of tiny Zions is an important precursor to the return of Enoch's city. The creation of the modern-day Zion will undoubtedly look different than the Zion planned by the early Saints. But the commandment to build Zion has never been withdrawn by the Lord. But it all starts with individuals who reach out to others and create relationships based on Philia - the love that is friendship.

In a beautiful demonstration of divine symmetry, the first Zion built by Enoch and the final Zion built by the Saints of the latter-days will come together in a glorious reunion. The covenant communities built by Enoch, Melchizedek, and others will meet the covenant communities built on earth by good people who reach out to those around them. A revelation given to Joseph Smith in 1832 includes a song that the inhabitants of the latter-day Zions and the Zions of former days will sing together, which reads in part: "*The Lord hath redeemed his people;And Satan is bound and time is no longer. The Lord hath gathered all things in one. The Lord hath brought down Zion from above. The Lord hath brought up Zion from beneath*" (Doctrine and Covenants 84:100).

But this grand and glorious reunion between the Saints of ancient days and the Latter-day Saints will not come to pass until we do the ground work of build our friendships down here on earth. The Church is designed to help us do this. The work of finding ways to assist and bless our ministering families naturally leads us to find Philia in our own wards and branches. Elder Jeffrey R. Holland described the work of ministering in terms closely equating it with Philia: "Brothers and sisters, we have a heaven-sent opportunity as an entire Church to demonstrate "pure religion … undefiled before God"—"to bear one another's burdens, that they may be light" and to "comfort those that stand in need of comfort," to minister to the widows and the fatherless, the married and the single, the strong and the distraught, the downtrodden and the robust, the happy and the sad—in short, all of us, every one of us, because *we all need to feel the warm hand of friendship* and hear the firm declaration of faith."[38]

38 Jeffrey R. Holland, "Be With and Strengthen Them," April 2018 General Conference, emphasis added.

## The Water of Life

I love to take people to the desert. I grew up in that environment and see its unique beauty. I often take people I want to get know better on adventures into the desert to hike, explore, and find the natural wonders that often can't be seen easily in the stark landscape. On a recent trip to the desert I was traveling with some friends, we came across a natural spring with crystal clear water. It wasn't difficult to find the spring because life grew all around it. Everything from moss to towering trees surrounded the spring, contrasting it with the desert landscape. We jumped in, swam for a few hours, and went on our journey refreshed and ready to traverse more of the desert landscape.

As we travel the spiritual deserts of mortality, friendship is the water we so desperately need to sustain our life. When we find friendship we find the power to put down roots and build covenant communities that can in turn house more refugees from spiritual deserts we wander in during our time on earth. Life and community spring from the Philia we work to develop with those around us. It happens quietly and sometimes just little acts of direction are needed to steer our energy toward creating the streams of friendship that will heal give meaning to our lives and open our doors of understanding. The healing waters of Philia, of friendship, fall like rain from heaven and also rise like a spring from the hearts of men and women in the latter days.

# Interlude: A Keeper of Sheep and a Tiller of the Ground

The story of Adam and Eve becomes fragmentary after they leave the Garden of Eden. Because of Latter-day revelation we know an angel appeared to them and soothed the curses of Eden by teaching of the blessings of the Atonement of Jesus Christ. Afterward both Adam and Eve praised God for His plan for their redemption. Those words become more poignant when the next story is told.

As commanded, Adam and Eve started their family. "Adam knew his wife, and she bare unto him sons and daughters, and they began to multiply and replenish the earth" (Moses 5:2). Adam and Eve recede into the background as the story becomes about each one of us. Of the first generation, only three are mentioned by name: Cain, Abel, and Seth.

We do not know if Cain was the first son of Adam and Eve, though he is usually presented as such when the story is told. We do not know if Abel was the first of their children to die, though it is presented as the first deliberate killing. It is not difficult to imagine the feelings of Adam and Eve when they found their child, bloodied and broken, slain by the hand of one of their other children. While it isn't difficult to imagine their sorrow, we might struggle to conceive of the shock Adam and Eve must have felt at seeing death for the first time. This was what the Father had tried to prepare them for. They would know the love that comes naturally from raising a child, but also the deep sorrow that comes from losing a child. This was death, a concept explained to them in the Garden. Yet for all of our preparation, parents then and now can never really be prepared for the loss of a child.

Eve's words recorded in the Book of Moses become particularly poignant when they are considered in the light of Abel's murder. "Were it not for our transgression we never should have had seed, and never should have known good and evil, and the joy of our redemption, and the eternal life which God giveth unto all the obedient" (Moses 5:11). The passage makes clear that in embracing mortality, Eve also knowingly embraced good and bad, joy and sorrow. It is comforting for us to know that as Adam and Eve buried their slain child they also knew they would see him again. They knew of redemption and eternal life through the Atonement of Jesus Christ. So which child was the cause of more sorrow to Adam and Eve? The one laying slain in a field or the one who carried out the horrendous act? The scriptures record simply, "Adam and Eve mourned before the Lord, because of Cain and his brethren" (Moses 5:28).

In this life, the greatest happiness and the greatest sorrows come from Storge, or the love of family. In our family members we most fully experience both the curses and the blessings of mortality. We rejoice in their success and offer comfort in their sorrow. With all people, but especially with our family members, we come to see things the way God sees them. Elder Dale G. Renlund taught, "to effectively serve others we must see them through a parent's eyes, through Heavenly Father's eyes. Only then we can we begin to comprehend the true worth of a soul."[39] It is through the soul-stretching agony of our family love, Storge, that we learn to become like our Heavenly Parents.

39 Dale G. Renlund, "Through God's Eyes," *Ensign*, October 2015, https://www.churchofjesuschrist.org/study/general-conference/2015/10/through-gods-eyes.

# Storge

*"That same sociality which exists among us here will exist among us there, only it will be coupled with eternal glory."*
—Joseph Smith Jr.

In April 1843, Joseph Smith traveled with two friends, Apostle Orson Hyde and his secretary William Clayton, to a small Latter-day Saint settlement twenty miles east of Nauvoo called Ramus. The Prophet traveled to Ramus to stay with a friend, Benjamin Johnson, and to visit his sister Sophronia McCleary. It was early spring, and several inches of snow fell the next day, but it had mostly melted away as the Saints in Ramus gathered to listen to their leaders. Orson Hyde preached a fiery sermon in which he spoke about the coming of the Savior, saying, "When He shall appear, we shall be like Him &c. He will appear on a white horse as a warrior, and maybe shall have some of the same spirit. Our God is a warrior." He added, "It is our privilege to have the Father and the Son dwelling in our hearts."[40] Later, as they dined at Sophronia's home, Joseph asked if he could offer some corrections to Elder Hyde's discourse, to which Elder Hyde re-

40 "Instruction, 2 April 1843, as Reported by Willard Richards," p. 35, The Joseph Smith Papers, https://www.josephsmithpapers.org/paper-summary/instruction-2-april-1843-as-reported-by-willard-richards/1

plied, "They shall be thankfully received." Joseph proceeded to correct Elder Hyde by saying, "When he [the Savior] shall appear we shall see him as he is. We shall see that he is a man like ourselves. And that same sociality which exists among us here shall exist among us there, only it will be coupled with eternal glory which glory we do not now enjoy."[41] "Sociality" is a broad word that can refer to any kind of human interaction, but it appears at that time that Joseph Smith had a specific kind of human relationship in mind. He was about to bring Storge, loosely translated as the love of family, into the eternal realms.

A few weeks later Joseph once again visited Ramus and stayed with his friend Benjamin Johnson. Benjamin later recalled, "In the evening he called me and my wife to come and sit down, for he wished to marry us according to the Law of the Lord." Benjamin responded incredulously. "I thought it a joke, and said I should not marry my wife again, unless she courted me, for I did it all the first time." But Joseph persisted, with Benjamin noting, "He chided my levity, told me he was in earnest, and so it proved, for we stood up and were sealed by the Holy Spirit of Promise."[42] In small ceremonies like this, mostly carried out in the last few years of Joseph Smith's life, Storge became fully realized as one of the most meaningful parts of the religion of the Latter-day Saints.

The Saints in Joseph Smith's day believed with all their hearts that Jesus Christ had overcome death. They knew they would live again. But the question that seemed to linger in their hearts was, what kind of life will I lead in the eternities? Most Christians (now and then) believe that family relationships are important in this life but will not exist in the eternities. A dictionary of orthodox Christian theology I keep in my office plainly states that "neither sex nor family is absolute . . . The more we commend the family, the more we must acknowledge that no human institution can be translated straight into heaven."[43]

---

41 "Journal, December 1842–June 1844; Book 2, 10 March 1843–14 July 1843," p. 37, The Joseph Smith Papers, https://www.josephsmithpapers.org/paper-summary/journal-december-1842-june-1844-book-2-10-march-1843-14-july-1843/45

42 Benjamin F. Johnson, *My Life's Review* (Independence, MO: Zion's Printing and Publishing, 1947), 93.

43 Helen Oppenheimer, "Theology of Marriage," *The Westminster Dictionary of Christian Theology*, ed. Alan Richardson and John Bowden, (Philadelphia: The Westminster Press, 1983), 346-347.

In contrast to this the Lord revealed to the Latter-day Saints that family *is* absolute, and the family does translate directly into heaven. Further, the best way for us to understand and comprehend God is to appreciate that our relationship with Him is familial. He is not just our Creator, but our Father in a very literal sense. The Prophet Joseph F. Smith taught, "Who are there besides the Latter-day Saints who contemplate the thought that beyond the grave we will continue in the family organization? the father, the mother, the children recognizing each other in the relations which they owe to each other and in which they stand to each other? this family organization being a unit in the great and perfect organization of God's work, and all destined to continue throughout time and eternity?"[44]

In contrast to almost the entire Christian world, Latter-day Saints believe that family relationships *do* transcend our earthly existence and continue into heaven and the eternities. In fact, our familial love forms the very ground that successful relationships in this life and the next are built upon. Far from being an earthly institution - a "til' death do us part" kind of arrangement - family is the bedrock of human relationships before this life, during this life, and in the life beyond. This familial love, at times misunderstood in the teachings of other Christian faiths, is as important to our happiness and stability as the ground we choose to build our life and homes upon.

## What Is Storge?

In *The Four Loves*, C. S. Lewis calls Storge "the humblest and most widely diffused of loves, the love which in our experience seems to differ least from that of the animals." He also praises it as "the least discriminating of the loves."[45] For the most part, Lewis simplifies Storge to simple affection for people or things. In a Greek lexicon, Storge is typically defined as family love, or the bond between mothers, fathers, sons, daughters, sisters, and brothers.[46] It is in elevating the importance of Storge that Latter-day Saints make perhaps their most valuable contribution to the theolo-

44 *Teachings of the Presidents of the Church: Joseph F. Smith*, (Salt Lake City: The Church of Jesus Christ of Latter-day Saints, 1998, 2011), Chapter 43: Fathers in the Home.

45 Lewis, *The Four Loves*, 31–32.

46 Jack Zavada, "What is Storge?" *Learn Religions*, https://www.learnreligions.com/what-is-storge-love-700698

gy of the larger Christian world. When Joseph Smith taught that "the same sociality which exists among us here will exist among us there," he elevated Storge from being a pleasant part of mortal life to an essential part of our eternal life.

Storge might be the most simple, and the least noticeable of loves, but only because we take it for granted. In earlier chapters we likened the transfixing nature of Eros to fire, and the nourishing character of Philia to water. In contrast to these first two loves, Storge is more constant and stable. We take it for granted because it is like the earth under our feet. Our family loves are the first connections we form in this life because it is the reason for this life, the very reason the world we live in was created. President Russell M. Nelson taught, "Grand as it is, planet Earth is part of something even grander—that great plan of God. Simply summarized, the earth was created that families might be."[47] Storge, like the earth, is constantly there, offering its gifts to sustain us and provide us with the resources we need to survive. It is more dependable than the other loves just like earthquakes are much rarer than fires or floods. But when upheaval comes within our family lives, just like an earthquake it can result in devastating consequences.

In elevating Storge in this way, the early Saints went against the grain of centuries of Christian thought. The majority of Christian religions teach that marriage and familial relationships are dissolved after this life. One religious group writes, "Isn't marriage the most profound institution God created for humanity? Isn't the bond between husband and wife meant to be the most intimate, treasured relationship in this life? How can heaven be heaven without it? . . . Just as a lamp is unnecessary in the light of the sun, so the sun itself will be unnecessary in the light of God. And so it will be with the marriages of this present world, fleeting as they are and inevitably severed when death do us part."[48]

In contrast to this, the revelations of the Restoration teach a different truth about familial love. Robert D. Hales taught, "The family is not an accident of mortality. It existed as an organizational unit in the heavens before the world was formed; historically, it started on earth with Adam and Eve, as recorded in Genesis. Adam and Eve were married and sealed for time and all eternity by the Lord, and as a result their family will exist eter-

47 Russell M. Nelson, "The Creation," *Ensign*, April 2000, https://www.churchofjesuschrist.org/study/general-conference/2000/04/the-creation

48 Subby Szertzsky, "Why Is There No Marriage in Heaven?" *Focus on the Family*, https://www.focusonthefamily.ca/content/why-is-there-no-marriage-in-heaven

nally."[49] Rather than seeing familial love as an earthly condition, the revelations of the Restoration elevate Storge as a key part of our existence before we came to earth and a vital facet of the afterlife.

### Storge and the Nature of God

In a sermon given near the end of his life, the Prophet Joseph Smith declared, "I want to ask this congregation, every man, woman, and child, to answer in their own hearts, what kind of being God is?" It was a bold question to ask in 1844, and it remains a bold question ask today. But the Prophet was unflinching in his request that everyone think deeply about the nature of God. "If men do not comprehend the character of God, they do not comprehend themselves," he added.[50] In seeking to comprehend the character of God, a thousand questions spring to mind. Who is He? Why does He care about us so much? Why does His connection to human beings seem to hold precedence over His connection to all of his other creations?

Joseph answered his own question in short order. "God Himself was once as we are now, and is an exalted man, and sits enthroned in yonder heavens! . . . if you were to see Him today, you would see Him like a man in form—like yourselves in all the person image and very form as a man." Why is this critical knowledge for a man or woman to know? "Having a knowledge of God, we begin to know how to approach Him, and how to ask so as to receive an answer. When we understand the character of God, and know how to come to Him, He begins to unfold the heavens to us, and to tell us all about it. When we are ready to come to Him, He is ready to come to us."[51] The last great teaching of Joseph Smith's life was that God and man are the same kind of being, just in different stages of their progression. We aren't just a creation of God. We are His family.

In no way does this teaching diminish the glory and power of God; it is meant to elevate the minds of His sons and daughters. Elder Tad R. Callister taught, "The difference between man and God is significant—but it is one of degree, not kind. It is the difference between an acorn and an oak

---

49 Robert D. Hales, "The Family: A Proclamation to the World," in *Clothed with Charity: Talks from the 1996 Women's Conference*, ed. Dawn Hall Anderson (Salt Lake City, UT: Deseret Book, 1997), 134.

50 *Teachings of Presidents of the Church: Joseph Smith* (Salt Lake City, UT: Intellectual Reserve, 2007), 36–44.

51 *Teachings of the Presidents*, 36–44.

tree, a rosebud and a rose, a son and a father."[52] The last comparison made by Elder Callister is the most powerful, because in the end, our connection to God is greater than just being the same kind of being; it is a familial connection, a father-child relationship. An address to fathers published by the Quorum of the Twelve Apostles in 1973 declared, "It is significant that of all the titles of respect and honor and admiration that are given to Deity, He has asked us to address Him as Father."[53]

Knowing we are part of God's family and that He loves us as a Father leads to another distinct teaching: A Mother in Heaven. The earliest known reference to this teaching in the Restoration came in 1839 when Zina Huntington was grieving the loss of her mother. She approached Joseph Smith, asking, "Will I know my mother when I get over on the other side?" "Certainly you will," the Prophet replied, "More than that, you will meet and become acquainted with your eternal Mother, the wife of your Father in Heaven." Zina was astonished, asking, "And then I have a Mother in Heaven?" to which Joseph replied, "You assuredly have. How could a Father claim His title unless there were also a Mother to share that parenthood?"[54] In another instance recorded by Abraham H. Cannon, Joseph Smith invited Sidney Rigdon and Zebedee Coltrin to accompany him into the woods to pray. According to Cannon, after their prayer, the small group experienced a series of four visions. The men "saw a brilliant light surrounding a pedestal which seemed to rest on the earth. They closed their eyes again and prayed. They then saw, on opening them, Father seated upon a throne; they prayed again and on looking saw the Mother also; and after praying and looking the fourth time they saw the Savior added to this group."[55]

---

52 Tad R. Callister, "Our Identity and Our Destiny," Education Week Devotional, August 14, 2012, https://speeches.byu.edu/talks/tad-r-callister/our-identity-and-our-destiny/

53 "Father, Consider Your Ways," Ensign, June 2002, https://www.churchofjesuschrist.org/study/ensign/2002/06/father-consider-your-ways?lang=eng

54 Susa Young Gates, *History of the Young Ladies' Mutual Improvement Association of the Church of Jesus Christ of Latter-day Saints* (Salt Lake City, UT: Deseret News, 1911), 15–16. Susa Young Gates recalled being told the story personally by Zina Huntington Young.

55 Abraham H. Cannon Journal, August 25, 1880, quoted in Linda P. Wilcox, "The Mormon Concept of a Mother in Heaven," in *Sisters in Spirit: Mormon Women in Historical and Cultural Perspective*, ed. Maureen Ursenbach Beecher and Lavina Fielding Anderson (Urbana: University of Illinois Press, 1987), 64–77

During Joseph Smith's lifetime, teaching about a Heavenly Mother appears to have been shared privately among his close associates. After his death, teachings about the doctrine began to appear in Church publications. In a poem published in the *Times and Seasons* in January 1845, W.W. Phelps wrote, "Come to me; here's they myst'ry that man hath not seen; Here's our Father in heaven, and Mother, the Queen; Here are worlds that have been, and the worlds yet to be; Here's eternity,—endless; amen: Come to Me."[56] A few months later Eliza R. Snow published a poem entitled "My Father In Heaven," today known as "O My Father," which reads, "In the heav'ns are parents single? No, the thought makes reason stare; Truth is reason—truth eternal, Tells me I've a mother there."[57]

In the years following, the teaching of Heavenly Parents became an important teaching in the Latter-day Saint doctrine. In 1909 a message from the First Presidency taught, "All men and women are in the similitude of the universal Father and Mother and literally the sons and daughters of deity."[58] In 1991, Gordon B. Hinckley, then a counselor in the First Presidency taught, "Logic and reason would certainly suggest that if we have a Father in Heaven, we have a Mother in Heaven. That doctrine rests well with me."[59] Four years later, the Family Proclamation was introduced to the Church, which reads, "All human beings—male and female—are created in the image of God. Each is a beloved spirit son or daughter of heavenly parents, and as such, each has a divine nature and destiny."[60] These are just a small sampling of teachings that demonstrate why familial love is so important to the beliefs of the Latter-day Saints. President Dallin H. Oaks summed up the centrality of this doctrine when he taught, "Our theology begins with heavenly parents. Our highest aspiration is to be like them."[61]

While belief in a divine masculine and divine feminine are important to Latter-day Saints, Church leaders have been cautious with this teaching. Church members worship Heavenly Father in the name of Jesus Christ and do not pray to Heavenly Mother. President Hinckley taught, "The fact that we do not pray to our Mother in Heaven in no way belittles or denigrates

---

56 W. W. Phelps, "Come to Me," *Times and Seasons* 6 (January 15, 1845): 783.

57 Eliza R. Snow, "My Father in Heaven," *Times and Seasons* 6 (November 15, 1845): 1039.

58 "The Origin of Man," *Improvement Era* 13, no. 1 (November 1909): 78.

59 Gordon B. Hinckley, "Daughters of God," *Ensign,* November 1991, 100.

60 "The Family: A Proclamation to the World," *Ensign* or *Liahona,* May 2017, 145.

61 Dallin H. Oaks, "Apostasy and Restoration," *Ensign*, May 1995, 84.

Her. None of us can add to or diminish the glory of Her."[62] What the doctrine of Heavenly Parents does do is assure us of the importance of feeling, learning, and sharing Storge on our journey to becoming more like the divine. Learning to feel familial love is learning to feel divine love. Elder Jeffrey R. Holland asked if mortals "can love so much and try so hard, what does that say of a more godly love that differs from our own as the stars differ from the sun? . . . What would this world's inhabitants pay to know that Heavenly Parents are reaching across those same streams and mountains and deserts, anxious to hold them close?"[63]

## Storge Means Nobody Gets Left Behind

Because of the delightful animated film *Lilo and Stitch,* most people are familiar with the term Ohana. Ohana is a term in the Hawaiian language that denotes kinship. While researchers have pointed out that Ohana is a modern word, in usage in the Hawaiian language for really only the last fifty years, the way Ohana is used in our modern culture expresses some important concepts.[64] In *Lilo and Stitch* the theme of the movie is presented in one simple line of dialogue, "Ohana means family, and family means no one gets left behind, or forgotten." This simple concept expresses one important facet of Storge, that the families we live in can be related to blood, adoptive, or based on those we choose to make our family.

The Latter-day Saint concept of the family is sometimes seen as exclusionary because so much of our thought is centered around marriage between a man and a woman. Marriage between a man and woman is "central to the creator's plan for the eternal destiny of His children."[65] But Storge goes beyond this type of marriage and embraces all different kinds of family. At its essence is the concept of the family or our Heavenly Parents, and the divine nature of all of God's children in the eternities. The theology surrounding the family is that connecting husbands and wives through sealing is only the beginning of the process. Eventually the goal is to connect *all* of Heavenly Father and Heavenly Mother's children back to them through

62 Gordon B. Hinckley, "Daughters of God," *Ensign,* November 1991, 100.

63 Jeffrey R. Holland, *However Long and Hard the Road* (Salt Lake City, UT: Deseret Book, 1985), 47.

64 See https://kenconklin.org/mediawiki/index.php?title=The_Word_'Ohana_Is_A_Modern_Invention, accessed November 22, 2022.

65 *he Family: A Proclamation to the World,* 1995, paragraph 1.

one grand chain of sealing ordinances. Brigham Young explained the purpose of sealing this way:

"When we come to . . . sealing ordinances [for the dead], ordinances pertaining to the holy Priesthood, to connect the chain of the Priesthood from Father Adam until now, by sealing children to their parents, being sealed for our forefathers, etc, they cannot be done without a temple."[66]

President Young's description of the great chain of sealing talks about parents and children, it does not say that being a parent is a requirement to be part of the chain. Our theology will permit all different kinds of people in a number of different situations to be sealed into the family of Adam and Eve, and then in turn to the family of our Heavenly Parents. In the end the Eternal Family that Latter-day Saints refer to is really only one family, and that family goes into the Celestial Kingdom together.

Misunderstanding this theology has sometimes caused good faithful people to believe that they cannot be part of the great family of God. In answer to this we must emphasize two points. First, every person is a part of God's family regardless of their race, religion, sexuality, gender orientation, or any other category. The message of the Restoration is that every person is known and loved by an Eternal Father and Mother. That is the birthright of every human being. Second, our Heavenly Parents have given an open invitation for everyone of their children to join the sealing chain, but they have to join of their own free will. Sealing is a voluntary covenant that cannot be forced onto anyone. We choose to be part of the sealed family of God by entering into a covenant relationship with Jesus Christ. The scriptures differentiate between all mankind, who are the children of Heavenly Parents, and those who enter into the sealed family. The second family is often referred to in the scripture as the "Church of the Firstborn" (see Doctrine and Covenants 76:64,71,94,102, 77:11; 78:21; 88:5; 93:22; 107:19).

## Storge and the Three Births

Another way to visualize our membership in the Church of the Firstborn is to employ an metaphor often used in the scriptures: birth. Taking into account our premortal, mortal, and postmortal states, each person must be born three times in order to enter into exaltation. Each of these

66 *he Teachings of Presidents of the Church: Brigham Young,* (Salt Lake City: The Church of Jesus Christ of Latter-day Saints, 1997), Chapter 41: Temple Ordinances.

births involve two parents, and in each we receive a gift that advances us on the path toward reaching our full potential. These births also allow us to make connections through Storge to individuals who will play a key role in our journey toward exaltation.

The first birth is our birth as a spirit. The Doctrine and Covenants teaches that all of us existed as intelligences before we were created as spirits. We frankly don't know that much about this state, but Doctrine and Covenants 93 reveals that "Intelligence, or the light of truth, was not created or made, neither indeed can be" and that "all truth is independent in that sphere which God has placed it, to act for itself, as all intelligence also; otherwise there is no existence," concluding, "Behold, here is the agency of man" (Doctrine and Covenants 93:29-31). So intelligence is eternal. In that sense you have been around as long as God has. And intelligence has always had some form of agency, meaning we have always possessed the power to make our own choices. God didn't just program us to do what he wants, he took an intelligence able to make its own choices and then gave it a gift that imbued us with greater agency: a spirit body.

Admittedly, our knowledge of this first birth are limited. But prophets ancient and modern have testified that we are the children of Heavenly Parents who are resurrected, exalted, perfect beings. We grew up with these perfect parents who loved us and wanted the best for us. They respected us enough to hold councils and ask for our input on family decisions. Having perfect parents does not mean perfect children. One child in our heavenly family became the embodiment of all that was good, and our Heavenly Parents chose Him to serve as our Savior and Redeemer. Now and then, He still represents the best case scenario for a member of the family. On the other hand, one of our siblings also became the embodiment of evil, the worst case scenario in the family. Our parents did everything they could to help us achieve our potential, but they also respected our agency. The love They felt for us, Storge, will always connect us to Them.

At a certain point we reached a plateau in our progression and this is where the second birth comes into the plan. The next stop on our road to exaltation came in receiving a second gift, a physical body. Admittedly, this was not the same kind of body our Heavenly Parents. This was a starter body, filled with all kinds of potential but also given a limited lifespan. The parents involved in this birth are your earthly parents. Earthly parents are just as fallible as you and I are, and they often make mistakes. But for the most part parents love their children and work hard to give them a good life. Making us serve as parents was probably the greatest object lesson we could ever receive to help us understand the kind of love our Heavenly Parents have for us. Learning Storge, with all of its joys, was an important step on our journey. We also learned the frustrations and sorrows that can come when our children make suffer or make bad choices.

Our mortal life through the second birth is a gift that not all of our Parents' children qualified for. Abraham saw in vision that all of the family had the plan explained to them that Lucifer "was angry, and kept not his first estate; and, at that day, many followed after him" (Abraham 3:28). We do not know how many followed Lucifer, but it was a significant number. The scriptures often use the phrase a "third part" followed Lucifer, which has been erroneously interpreted to mean that one third of our family turned away from God and rejected the second birth. However the phrase "one third" never appears in scripture, but instead the phrase a "third part" which could be interpreted a number of different ways (see Revelation 12:4, 7-9; Doctrine and Covenants 29:36-37). The loss of their children must have deeply affected our Heavenly Parents, but their respect for agency was too great to force their children to take part in the second birth.

The third birth is often referred to as the new birth in the scriptures. Jesus explained this concept to Nicodemus, a member of the Jewish Sanhedrin, who came to visit in secret. Jesus told Nicodemus, "Except a man be born again, he cannot see the kingdom of God." Nicodemus confused the new birth with mortal birth, asking, "How can a man be born when he is old? Can he enter the second time into his mother's womb, and be born?" Jesus then clarified, "Except a man be born of water and of the Spirit, he cannot enter into the kingdom of God" (John 3:3-5).

The new birth, the third birth on our journey, is the final part of our transformation to become like God. Like mortal birth, it is preceded by a number of developmental steps before the final birth takes place. The birth of water, baptism, is just the first step on the journey. This process moves us through the other ordinances of the gospel, all gradual steps on our birth through the Holy Spirit. The final culmination is our resurrection, where we come forward with a perfect body and a perfect spirit. Jesus demonstrated all of the steps on this journey. During his mortal ministry he was undergoing the new birth, so he taught his disciples, "Be ye therefore perfect, even as your Father which is in heaven is perfect" (Matthew 5:48). After His resurrection, He slightly altered the phrase, declaring, "I would that ye should be perfect even as I, or your Father who is in heaven is perfect" (3 Nephi 12:48).

Our parents during the first two births are easily identified. Who then, are our parents during the new birth? Understanding this teaching helps clear up the roles of the Father and the Son. In a revelation given in 1831, Jesus declared, "To as many as received me, gave I power to become my sons; and even so will I give unto as many as will receive me, power to become my sons" (Doctrine and Covenants 38:4). In another revelation he emphasizes the same blessing for women, saying, "all who receive my gospel are sons and daughters in my kingdom" (Doctrine and Covenants 25:1). Heavenly Father is the Father of our spirits (Hebrews 12:9) but Jesus becomes the Father of our final birth unto eternal life?

However this leads to another question, who is the mother of our eternal life? Does the analogy break down at this point? The scriptures present a clear answer to this question, describing Jesus as having a wife. In Ephesians, Paul was counseling husbands and made a comparison to the Savior and his spouse, teaching, "Husbands, love your wives, even as Christ also loved the church, and gave himself for it" (Ephesians 5:25). Metaphorically, speaking, the Savior's spouse is the Church. I know that probably wasn't the answer you were looking for, but the scriptures don't present definitive information on whether or not Jesus was married during his mortality. We all have our pet theories, but the key teaching is that the Church was set up as the Savior's partner in bringing about our last birth into eternal life.

To justify this analogy further, in the Book of Revelation - a highly symbolic text - John sees a beautiful woman "clothed with the sun, and the moon under her feet, and upon her head a crown of twelve stars" (Revelation 12:1). The woman is shown to be with child, and threatened by a great red dragon with seven heads, representing Lucifer and his followers. The Joseph Smith Translation of this passage identifies the women and her child, explaining, "The dragon prevailed not against Michael, neither the child, nor the woman *which was the church of God,* who had been delivered of her pains, and brought forth the kingdom of our God and his Christ" (JST Revelation 12:7).

In the metaphor, Christ becomes the Father of our third birth with the Church acting as our mother. The Church nourishes us, teaches us, and guides us to make the right choices. You might not always agree with your mother, but most of us would never doubt that our mother has our best intentions toward us. In this way, the Church is an instrument God uses to teach us Storge, that familial love, for anyone who joins the covenant of Christ with us. There is a reason why in the Church we used the language of Storge to communicate closeness and connection. When we call someone "brother" or "sister" we emphasis the warm, nurturing care we should provide for everyone who joins us in the faith.

Through my Church service, I also learned how one of the most valuable things the Church does is provide surrogate families for people who lose family members through death, divorce, or other challenges we face in life. The people in our wards and branches can act as surrogates for missing fathers, mothers, or big brothers and sisters who nurture children as they grow into adulthood. You might remember the old saying that "it takes a village to raise a child." The language of Storge reminds us that your ward or branch is not just a group of people loosely connected by geography, but a small part of the larger family of God.

## Interlude: "I Have Been Pondering Sister Lydia's Lonely Condition"

Lydia Goldwaite was no stranger to complexity or sorrow in family life. Sent away to boarding school when she was fifteen, she met a man named Calvin Bailey and fell in love. They were married in 1828, when Lydia was just sixteen years old. Her union with Calvin proved to be difficult. Calvin drank excessively and became abusive towards Lydia. She was comforted by the birth of a daughter, Roseanna. "This great blessing soothed the aching heart of the youthful mother," she later wrote.[67]

Unfortunately, more sorrow came quickly when Lydia gave birth to a son, Edwin, who died almost immediately after birth. Soon after Calvin abandoned Lydia and their daughter. Lydia was left with no choice but to move home with her parents. A year later, her little girl became ill and passed away. By the time she was only twenty-one years old, Lydia had already lost two children, and her marriage was over.

67 See Nicolas J. Frederick, "God Rules! Lydia Goldthwaite Knight, 1812-1884," in *Women of Faith in the Latter Days,* ed. Richard E. Turley and Brittany A. Chapman, (Salt Lake City, UT: Deseret Book, 2011), 143-154.

After the death of her daughter, Lydia traveled to Mount Pleasant, Canada, to stay with the family of Freeman and Eliza Nickerson, friends of her parents. Despite all of the loss she had suffered, Lydia retained her faith in Jesus Christ. She wrote she looked forward to a meeting in the next life with "my dear children that have gone before me."[68]

In October 1833 Lydia received word of a man claiming to be a prophet with a new book of scripture, brought forth by the power of God. A few days later she met with Joseph Smith and Sidney Rigdon, who had come to the area to preach. At the time Joseph and Sidney were experiencing great anxiety over the safety of their own families, and their friends in Missouri, who were experiencing serious persecution. The Lord gave them a revelation to soothe their fears, telling them, "My friends Sidney and Joseph, your families are well; they are in mine hands, and I will do with them as seemeth me good; for in me there is all power" (Doctrine and Covenants 100:1). But the Lord also emphasized the importance of their preaching in the area, declaring, "I, the Lord, have suffered you to come unto this place; for thus it was expedient in me for the salvation of souls" (Doctrine and Covenants 100:4).

As Lydia listened to the teachings of Joseph and Sidney she was deeply moved. She later recorded that as she heard Joseph Smith tell of the coming forth of the Book of Mormon, she "saw his face become white and shining[,] glow seemed to beam from every feature."[69] She was baptized just a few days after she first heard the Prophet preach. Lydia's biography records that when she was baptized a few days later, she cried out while standing in the freezing water, "Glory to God in the highest. Thanks be to His holy name that I have lived to see this day."[70] At a meeting held the night of her baptism Lydia was caught up in the Spirit and spoke in tongues. According to her biography, "she was enveloped as with a flame, and, unable longer to retain her seat,

68 Lydia Bailey to Jesse and Sally Goldthwaite, June 22, 1833, Letters and Papers of Lydia Knight and Newel Knight, L. Tom Perry Special Collections, Harold B. Lee Library, Brigham Young University, referred to hereafter as Knight Papers.

69 William G. Hartley, *Stand By My Servant Joseph: The Story of the Joseph Knight Family and the Restoration*, (Provo, UT; Salt Lake City, UT: The Joseph Fielding Smith Institute for Latter-day Saint History, Deseret Book, 2003), 214.

70 Lydia Knight and Susa Young Gates, *Lydia Knight's History,* Noble Women's Life's Series 1 (Salt Lake City, UT: Juvenile Instructor Office, 1883), 11.

she arose and her mouth was filled with the praises of God and His glory. The spirit of tongues was upon her, and she was clothed in a shining light, so bright that all present saw it with great distinctness above the light of the fire and the candles."[71]

While she was overjoyed, with the manifestations of the Spirit she experienced, Lydia also worried over the place of woman abandoned by her husband in her new church. Would she been shunned or looked down upon because of her marital history? Joseph Smith was sensitive to her concerns. Before he left to return to his own family, he sat down with Lydia, saying, "I have been pondering on Sister Lydia's lonely condition, and wondering why it is that she has passed through so much sorrow and affliction and is thus separated from all her relatives. I now understand it. The Lord has suffered it even as he allowed Joseph of old to be afflicted, who was sold by his brethren as a slave to a far country, and through that became a savior to his house and country. Even so shall it be with her, the hand of the Lord will overrule it for good to her and her father's family." Joseph then spoke to Lydia directly, saying, "Sister Lydia, great are your blessings. The Lord, your Savior, loves you and will overrule all your past afflictions for good unto you."[72]

A few years later Lydia moved to Kirtland, where she met and fell in love with Newel Knight, one of Joseph Smith's close friends. Their marriage was personally performed by Joseph Smith. During the ceremony Joseph told them that marriage "was an institution of heaven first solemnized in the garden of Eden by God himself, by the authority of everlasting priesthood."[73]

Less than a year after their marriage, Lydia was given a patriarchal blessing by Joseph Smith, Sr. In the blessing she was promised, "The Lord loves thee and has given thee a kind and loving companion for thy comfort and your souls shall be knit together and nothing shall be able to dissolve them; neither distress nor death shall separate you." She was also promised, "Thou shalt be a mother to many children and thou

71 Hartley, 216.
72 Hartley, 217.
73 Hartley, 224.

shalt teach them righteousness and have power to keep them from the power of the destroyer."[74]

Lydia and Newel remained close companions and had seven children together before Newel's death in 1847 during the trek west. Even after his death, their bond remained strong. During her distress after his death, Lydia cried out, "Oh Newel, why has thou left me!" At that moment he appeared to her as a spirit, saying, "Be calm, let not sorrow overcome you. It was necessary that I should go . . . You cannot fully comprehend it now; but the time will come when you shall know why I left you and our little ones. Therefore, dry up your tears. Be patient, I will go before you and protect you in your journeyings."[75]

Lydia traveled on to Utah, where she endured and died in the faith in St. George in 1880.[76] Lydia Knight's story illustrates that family life in the Church has always been complex. Many people who feel like they cannot belong because they have experienced death, divorce, or other forms of complexity in their families feel like they cannot belong in a faith so centered around family. But the Church of Jesus Christ is not only meant to help us create strong families, but to provide a surrogate family for those without one. Like Lydia Knight, the blessings that the Lord has in store for us may take time to come, but while we wait He has provided us with a loving family of faith to help meet our needs.

### Storge and the Unmarried, Widowed, and Divorced

As mentioned early, one of the great misunderstandings of the theology of the Church is that it is exclusionary, when really it is meant to be the ultimate form of inclusion. Storge is not just intended for those who are in traditional husband/wife relationships. Our theology is inclusive enough to bring everyone into the family. There are times when the circumstances of our lives can make us fell like we don't fit into the Church, but there is a way for everyone to be part of the family of God and feel His love. Our theology naturally causes us to gravitate towards what has been called the nuclear family - one husband, one wife, and their children. But we need to

---

74 "Patriarchal Blessing of Lydia Knight," in *Early Patriarchal Blessings of The Church of Jesus Christ of Latter-day Saints,* ed. H. Michael Marquardt, (Salt Lake City, UT: Smith-Petit Foundation, 2007), 142.

75 Knight and Gates, *Lydia Knight's History,* 71-72.

76 Lydia Goldthwaite McClellan, Biography, Joseph Smith Papers.

become more accustomed to speaking in terms that are more inclusive of those in our family who don't fit easily into those categories.

We have liked Storge to the earth beneath our feet. When upheavals do come in our family life, it can feel like the ground beneath our feet has shifted. Storge is such a stabilizing force in our lives that something like the end of a marriage can make be as devastating to our emotional and mental health as an earthquake can be to our physical surroundings. But in the latter-days seismic events in our family lives are becoming more and more common, and whether you have experience one of these events or not, you will certainly see these aftershocks in your own lives or the lives of your loved ones.

Elder Gerrit W. Gong pointed out a significant change happening in the Church that might necessitate a change in the way we talk about family. He pointed out that "the majority of adult Church members are now unmarried, widowed, or divorced. This is a significant change. It includes more than half our Relief Society sisters and more than half our adult priesthood brothers. This demographic pattern has been the case in the worldwide Church since 1992 and in the Church in the United States and Canada since 2019."[77]

It can be difficult for a person who is unmarried, widowed, or divorced to feel like they fit into the theology of the Church. But when a person finds themselves in one of these categories, it becomes *more* important to draw them into the family of God. Storge has never been linked exclusively to blood relations, and neither is the sealing power that brings us into God's family. Elder Gong taught, "Our standing before the Lord and in His Church is not a matter of our marital status but of our becoming faithful and valiant disciples of Jesus Christ. Adults want to be seen as adults and to be responsible and contribute as adults. Disciples of Jesus Christ come from everywhere, in every shape, size, hue, and age, each with talents, righteous desires, and immense capacities to bless and serve. We seek daily to follow Jesus Christ with faith unto repentance and enduring joy."[78]

In addition, it is important for us to recognize that while sin can be the cause of divorce, most people who are involved in divorce are innocent victims. President Dallin H. Oaks taught, "There are many good Church members who have been divorced . . . We know that many of you are inno-

77 Gerrit W. Gong, "Room at the Inn," April 2021 General Conference.
78 Gerrit W. Gong, "Room at the Inn," April 2021 General Conference.

cent victims—members whose former spouses persistently betrayed sacred covenants or abandoned or refused to perform marriage responsibilities for an extended period. Members who have experienced such abuse have first-hand knowledge of circumstances worse than divorce. When a marriage is dead and beyond hope of resuscitation, it is needful to have a means to end it."[79] Divorce can be a difficult reality that many of us are tasked to navigate, but Storge can still exist, even in the midst of such difficult trials.

I remember when I was serving as an ecclesiastical leader meeting with one of the most compassionate and Christlike people in our ward. She and her husband were married in the temple, but several years into their marriage things became very difficult. Her husband struggled with depression and his testimony of the Gospel. He was unfaithful to her, and though she forgave him, they still struggled. They had one child, and they stayed together, both acting as loving parents to him. She came to me asking for held when she found out that her husband had been unfaithful again. We talked for a long time about what her options were. I told her that I couldn't make the decision for her, but that I thought she was justified if she felt the need to end her marriage. Not able to come to a decision, we both agreed to take a little more time for thought and prayer, and then meet again.

When we met again, she told me that she felt strongly that she needed to give her husband six more months. I was surprised but told her I would support her no matter what she chose to do. I wish I could say that six months later we met and everything in their marriage was fixed. But the truth is that what she really gained in those six months was a strong confirmation from the Savior that she had done everything she possibly could to save her marriage, and it was time to move on. She got a divorce and resolved that she would just focus the rest of her life on raising her son. She didn't really think she would marry again, and after her experience she wasn't looking for someone.

Over the next few years a few interesting things happened. One of the counselors in our bishopric received a prompting that this sister should serve as the president of the primary in our ward. When her name was brought up in ward council meetings, no one even mentioned her divorce because we all knew what a wonderful person she was. The only person who expressed any concerns about this calling was this sister herself, but I assured her that the Lord knew she was qualified. She turned out to be one of the

79 Dallin H. Oaks, "Divorce," April 2007 General Conference.

best primary presidents I have ever seen. She was overflowing with Storge for the children in our ward. She had always wanted a large family with a lot of children, and now she had one. She knew every child by name, and had a gift for helping them feel loved and needed. She became a mother to all the children of the ward, including my own.

About a year and a half after her divorce she set up an appointment to meet with me. I was always happy to see her, but this time she had a coy smile that made me feel like she was hiding a secret. Once I closed the door she couldn't hold back any more. "I'm in love" she told me. I listened to her story and heard about how she met a man whose story was similar to her own. For years he struggled in a very challenging marriage. He did everything he could to save the marriage, but finally it was time to move on. He divorced and tried to move on with his life. With the way she talked about him I thought he sounded a little too good to be true. We had grown close and I was a little protective so I asked if I could meet with him. I thought maybe she was so lovestruck that she might not be using her best judgment.

When I met with him I was soon surprised to find out that he really was just as wonderful as she had described him! He spoke at length about how hard he tried to make his first marriage work, how much he loved his children from his marriage, and how devoted he was to the Gospel. Most importantly, he talked about how lucky he was to find her, and how he saw her as his chance at a fresh start. Both of them were still wary about entering into a new marriage, and so they asked me to perform a civil ceremony for them, which I did. I was also thrilled to be in the temple with them a year later when they were sealed for time and all eternity.

I don't mention this story as a way of suggesting that everyone who is unmarried will find someone as wonderful as this dear sister did. I am happy it worked out for them, but I recognize that in many cases good people who are single, widowed, or divorced don't find new love in this life. But Storge is something that we can find in a lot of places in this life. The structure of the Church is designed to give us a surrogate family if we look for those ways we can serve and love others. And even if we don't find those connections in life that we want, Storge, like all of the loves, is something that will definitely exist in the next life.

## Storge and LGBTQIA+

Another group that often feels cut off by the theology of the Restoration are those who identify as LGBTQIA+. That is a long and growing list of abbreviations, standing for Lesbian, Gay, Bisexual, Transgender, Queer, Intersex, Asexual, with a plus sign on the end just in case we missed anyone. Each of these categories features its own set of complexities, and their challenges can vary greatly. There is not a one size fits all approach to each of these circumstances. At times a person experiencing one of these identities often feels cut off from Storge, but this love can be even more important and affirming for a person, especially a young person who is sorting through their identity.

First, it is critical for a person who is working their way through issues linked to these questions of identity to feel that they are loved, first by their Heavenly Parents, and then by their earthly families. On a website created specifically by the Church for people who experience same-sex attraction, the first question is, "Does God love me?" The answer given is "God loves all of us. He loves those of different faiths and those without any faith. He loves those who suffer. He loves the rich and poor alike. He loves people of every race and culture, the married or single, and those who experience same-sex attraction or identify as gay, lesbian, or bisexual. And God expects us to follow His example."[80] In a devotional given at Brigham Young University that I attended in person, I remember the Prophet Russell M. Nelson teaching, "Because we feel the depth of God's love for His children, we care deeply about every child of God, regardless of age, personal circumstances, gender, sexual orientation, or other unique challenges."[81]

Second, people who find themselves in LGBTQIA+ categories need to feel love from their families here on earth. People, especially young people who are working their way through these questions, often feel isolated and alienated from their families. Family members can show love for these individuals without compromising their beliefs or values. This isn't just something we do to provide peace in our families, it is something the leaders of the Church have directly counseled us to do. A statement by President Dallin H. Oaks shows how to walk the line between love and law. He taught, "While God's commandments forbid all unchaste behavior and reaffirm

80 Same-Sex Attraction, churchofjesuschrist.org, accessed November 25, 2022.

81 Russell M. Nelson, "The Love and Laws of God," BYU Devotional, September 17, 2019.

the importance of marriage between a man and woman, the Church and its faithful members should reach out to individuals who are attracted to those of the same sex or whose sexual orientation or gender identity is inconsistent with their sex at birth."[82]

Storge can play a pivotal role in helping these individuals survive some of the hazards that can be a threat to their very lives. Social scientists have long been concerned about the rate of poor mental health, depression, or suicide among youth in these categories. In a recent study reviewing data among LGBQ youth in Utah found that religion was a factor in better mental health and lower suicide rates in this population. The study noted that for LGBQ youth, Latter-day Saints were significantly lower than those of other religions or no religion when it came to suicide ideation, meaning contemplating self-harm. Latter-day Saints were also significantly lower than all other religions when it came to depression. In one of the models presented in the study the rate for suicide ideation were as follows: Latter-day Saints: 28%; Catholic: 37%; Protestant: 46%; "Other": 50%; None: 49%. Rates of suicide attempts among LGBQ individuals from the study showed, Latter-day Saint: 10%; Catholic: 26%; Protestant: 25%; "Other": 30%; None: 23%.[83] While the suicide of any individual is a tragedy, the study shows the religious affiliation, especially among Latter-day Saints, was tied to lower rates of suicide ideation and suicide attempts.

In their efforts to explain these results, the researchers conducting this study tied these results to strong family ties. They wrote, "results suggest that, on average, Latter-day Saints (whether LGBQ or not) are lower in suicidality and depression because they have (again, on average) stronger family connections and less drug abuse. This suggests that independent of religious background, a youth with a strong family background and low levels of substance use will have lower suicidality and depression."[84] Among these individuals Storge can play a significantly role in alleviating these harmful risk factors. The researchers of this study directly state that "strong family connections are central to a lower risk of suicide."[85]

---

82 Dallin H. Oaks, "Women can serve as witnesses for baptism, temple sealings, President Nelson announces in policy change," *Church News,* October 2, 2019.

83 W. Justin Dyer, Michael A. Goodman, and David S. Wood, "Religion and Sexual Orientation as Predictors of Utah Youth Suicidality," *BYU Studies Quarterly 61,* no. 2, (2022*),* 69.

84 Dyer, Goodman, and Wood, 77.

85 Dyer, Goodman, and Wood, 77.

While this study only highlights LGBQ youth and not all of the groups we have brought up, it is easy to imagine that the benefits of showing Storge toward a child who wrestles with their gender identity, or who is working through questions of sexual identity would produce similar results. Helping these individuals know that they are part of a Heavenly Family and a loving family on earth can be an important part of helping them find joy, peace, and connection in this life and the next. Clearly, Storge is just as important for these groups as it is for everyone else, and perhaps even more so. So how do we develop and nourish Storge within our lives and families?

## Developing Storge in Our Lives

While Storge is a more stable form of love, like the ground beneath our feet it can become sterile and unproductive without constant nourishment and care. I grew up in a small farming community, and learned early that planting a seed, water it, and growing it is only a small part of the work. We must constant till and plow the soil, adding in elements that will provide nourishment to the life that draws its strength from the soil.

Because of our powerful theology of the family, Latter-day Saint leaders have spoken about family life more than almost any other subject. Statements from modern prophets like "No other success can compensate for failure in the home" or "the family that prays together stays together" find honored places on the walls of the homes where Latter-day Saint families live. My personal favorite quote comes from David O. McKay, who said, "Let husband and wife never speak to one another in loud tones, unless the house is on fire."[86] Perhaps the best encapsulation of all the counsel given by Church leaders is found in the Proclamation on the Family, which states simply: "Happiness in family life is most likely to be achieved when founded upon the teachings of the Lord Jesus Christ." This inspired proclamation goes on to list the building blocks of creating Storge within our own homes. "Successful marriages and families are established and maintained on principles of faith, prayer, repentance, forgiveness, respect, love, compassion, work, and wholesome recreational activities."[87]

---

86 David O. McKay, *Stepping Stones to an Abundant Life*, comp. Llewelyn R. McKay (Salt Lake City, UT: Deseret Book, 1971), 294

87 *The Family: A Proclamation to the World*, The Church of Jesus Christ of Latter-day Saints, https://www.churchofjesuschrist.org/study/scriptures/the-family-a-proclamation-to-the-world/the-family-a-proclamation-to-the-world?lang=eng

While I accept that it isn't possible to provide better counsel than is contained in the Family Proclamation, let me humbly suggest three practices that can help to implement these principles. I am describing things that have been successful in my family, which consists of my, my wife, and children ranging from twenty to four years old. But everything here can be adapted to you and your family, even if there is only one of you. This is also not a comprehensive list of good family practices, just three things to be particularly helpful in our family. You start anywhere, but here are three practices that have helped us develop Storge in our family:

1. Make time for family meals.
2. Establish a family culture for the Sabbath day.
3. Use councils to govern your family with love.

Let's look at each one of these separately.

## Storge and Family Meals

First, make time for family meals. A few years ago, President Dallin H. Oaks noted that "the number of those who report that their 'whole family eats dinner together' has declined 33 percent." President Oaks added, "This is most concerning because the time a family spends together 'eating meals at home [is] the strongest predictor of children's academic achievement and psychological adjustment." That statement struck me—were family meals really that important, or was President Oaks overselling his point? Did something as simple as family meals really qualify as the "strongest predictor" of academic achievement and psychological adjustment in children? President Oaks went on to suggest that "family mealtimes have also been shown to be a strong bulwark against children's smoking, drinking, or using other drugs."[88] I was intrigued by this, so I went on a few social science websites to see if family meals really were the source of so much academic study. What I found surprised me again. Not only was President Oaks speaking accurately, but he may have been *underselling* the importance of family meals! In short order I found dozens of studies about the impact of family meals on children. One study published in 2017 found that only 29.7% of children ages 12 to 17 ate meals 4 or 5 days a week with their

88 Dallin H. Oaks, "Good, Better, Best," *Ensign* or *Liahona*, October 2007, https://www.churchofjesuschrist.org/study/general-conference/2007/10/good-better-best?lang=eng

families. The researchers found "that involvement in family mealtimes has been positively associated with academic performance and negatively related to engagement in risky behavioral activities such as suicide, smoking, drinking alcohol, and using drugs." The researchers further found links between "more family meals and increased child engagement in school, lower levels of child problematic social behaviors, and higher levels of positive social skills."[89]

So many positive outcomes from something as mundane as a family meal might seem astounding. Sure, feeding your family regularly has nutritional benefits, but how can it affect so many things? In truth, it has nothing to do with food and everything to do with time. In a world where children and parents are becoming increasingly over scheduled, family meals are a proven way of promoting communication by allowing family members to "catch up on the events of the day, provide support, discuss news, tell stories, solve problems, have fun, and plan."[90]

I was so impressed by the number of studies reaching the same conclusion that I decided to do everything in my power to ensure we held at least one meal together daily. My wife and I have four children who were spaced out over a period of two decades. When we first began this experiment, it meant gathering together a sixteen year old, a fourteen year old, a five year old, and a one year old. It wasn't easy, and it didn't come without a lot of complaining. We discussed things as a family and decided to ban screens at the table, which was difficult, especially for me because of Church callings. Over a period of months, our family began to grow closer. Though our schedule was still filled with all manner of activities, we still felt connected. I heard every day about every one of my children's days, along with their triumphs, struggles, and worries. We didn't carry out a sociological study to determine the effectiveness of our experiment, but there is no doubt in my mind that we felt closer and more connected as a family.

The underlying principle here is that you need time to teach your children the principles taught in the Family Proclamation. For example, mealtimes became a great venue for showcasing the importance of prayer and seeing how members of the family prayed for each other. The kitchen and dining room are a good place to demonstrate faith, forgiveness, compassion,

89 Sharon D. Lawrence and Mary K. Plisco, "Family Mealtimes and Family Functioning," *The American Journal of Family Therapy* 45, no. 4 (2017), 195–96.

90 Lawrence and Plisco, 195.

or any of the other key teachings of the Savior. The time of day isn't as important as the time itself. Many families I work with have difficulty finding time in the evenings, so they eat a big breakfast together every day. The important thing is that there is a time with minimal distractions to help you learn, love, and develop your Storge together.

### Storge and the Sabbath Day

Second, establish a family culture around the Sabbath day. In my experience counseling and working with families, there is nothing that demonstrates a family's internal culture quite as much as their approach to the Sabbath day. When my wife and I developed our own family culture early in our marriage, there was no subject we clashed on quite as much as the Sabbath. We both grew up in wonderful, faithful families, and we both saw the Sabbath as sacred and important, but there were (and still are) quirks in the way we saw the Sabbath. For instance, my wife's family had a cabin near a lake where they spent a lot of time during the summer. During her time at the cabin, the family developed a rule that they did not swim on Sundays. A year or two into our marriage, we spent a few days at a hotel with my family. On a Sunday, I suggested we all relax by going down to the Jacuzzi in the hotel. My wife immediately objected, almost involuntarily saying, "We don't swim on Sunday." I replied that we weren't *swimming*; my plan was just to *sit* in warm water while we conversed as a family. What could be more appropriate than a simple family conversation on the Sabbath in a comfortable setting! Needless to say, we got into one of those arguments you aren't supposed to get into in front of your parents when you are newly wed. I also came to a realization: We hadn't quite worked out the Sabbath-day rules of our family culture yet.

In the weeks following, we did have a number of conversations about how we wanted to observe the Sabbath in our family. We searched the scriptures and the words of the prophets for guidance. One of the most valuable statements we found in developing our family culture came from President Russell M. Nelson, who taught, "How do we hallow the Sabbath day? In my much younger years, I studied the work of others who had compiled lists of things to do and things not to do on the Sabbath. It wasn't until later that I learned from the scriptures that my conduct and my attitude on the Sabbath constituted a sign between me and my Heavenly Father. With that understanding, I no longer needed lists of dos and don'ts." Like President Nelson, we initially looked for "dos" and "don'ts" about this particular commandment, rather than discussing a principle-based approach. "When I had to make a decision whether or not an activity was appropriate for the Sabbath, I simply asked myself, 'What sign do I want to give to God?' That question made my choices about the Sabbath day crystal clear."[91]

Impressed by President Nelson's principle-based approach to the Sabbath, we sat down as a couple and came up with a few principles of our own. We eventually formulated three questions to guide our Sunday activities:

1. Is it spiritual in nature?
2. Is absolutely necessary?
3. Is it providing love and/or service to someone?

We decided that if we could answer yes to one of the questions, it was a maybe. If we answered yes to two of the questions it was appropriate. And if we answered yes to all three it was *definitely* appropriate. One Sunday after we formulated the questions, my wife woke up very ill and asked me to go the store to buy some medicine. Instead of automatically replying "We don't go to the store on Sunday," I broke into a wide grin and slyly asked, "Is that spiritual in nature?" My wife replied weakly, "No." Then I asked, "Is it absolutely necessary?" She replied, "Yes!" Then I asked with mock sincerity, "Would I be providing love and/or service to you?" The look my wife gave me after this line of questioning indicated I was really pushing my luck. So, I went to the store, walked in wearing my Sunday suit, purchased the needed medicine, and walked out.

As our children joined our family we shared the questions with them. Over the years the questions became the springboard for a number of discussions about the Sabbath and what kind of sign we wanted to give to God through our worship. In our family councils, one of our children proposed a fourth question that we later adopted into our family culture: "Can we do this activity together as a family?" Her wise addition to our Sabbath standards led to invaluable experiences that helped us develop Storge within our family.

91 Russell M. Nelson, "The Sabbath is a Delight," *Ensign* or *Liahona*, April 2015, https://www.churchofjesuschrist.org/study/general-conference/2015/04/the-sabbath-is-a-delight

This discussion leads us to the third suggestion: Use councils to govern your family with love. One way to undermine the development of Storge in our families is to take a dictatorial approach toward familial governance. Family members who don't feel like they are listened to or valued in decision making can become resentful and bitter. Contrary to this, the Lord counsels leaders that "no power or influence can or ought to be maintained by virtue of the priesthood, only by persuasion, by long-suffering, by gentleness and meekness, and by love unfeigned; By kindness, and pure knowledge, which shall greatly enlarge the soul without hypocrisy, and without guile" (D&C 121:41–42). Holding regular family councils where every member of the family can have a voice builds trust, unity, and Storge.

President M. Russell Ballard has suggested that at least four types of family council can be utilized. "First, a general family council consisting of the entire family. Second, an executive family council consisting of a mother and father. Third, a limited family council consisting of parents and one child, [and] fourth, a one-on-one family council consisting of one parent and one child."[92] These councils can be simple and straightforward. You don't need to instruct your family in parliamentary procedure to conduct a family council! Properly conducted, a family dinner can serve as a family council. A car ride to take a child to dance or swimming lessons can serve as a family council. In our family, we got into the habit of pulling out a calendar at the beginning of our family scripture study on Sundays and coordinating everything that we needed to do during the week. Just knowing everyone's schedules reduced a lot of the drama in our family and increased the Storge we felt for each other.

What if you are single and don't have a family? The most important type of Storge we develop in this life is between ourselves, our Heavenly Parents, and our esteemed elder brother, Jesus Christ. A single person will undoubtedly feel the love of a concerned parent as they seek to "counsel with the Lord in all thy doings" (Alma 37:37). After all, the ultimate form of Storge is found by seeking to develop a familial relationship with our Heavenly Parents, our Elder Brother Jesus Christ, and all of our brothers and sisters here on earth.

---

92 M. Russell Ballard, "Family Councils," *Ensign* or *Liahona*, April 2016, https://www.churchofjesuschrist.org/study/general-conference/2016/04/family-councils

As mentioned, Storge is already such a powerful force in our lives that at times it can be taken for granted. It is true that familial love might be the most natural of the loves we feel, but it still must be treated carefully and nourished tenderly in all of our thoughts and actions. Just like a husband and a wife must deliberately seek time and space to develop their relationship, we must be deliberate in our work to build Storge among all family members. When I was in graduate school, one of my professors noted that he always took time during the week to spend twenty minutes doing someone one-on-one with each of his children that was meaningful to them. If the child was a teen, he took them for a drive or a milkshake. For younger children, it might mean playing with dolls or jumping on a trampoline for twenty minutes. At first, twenty minutes per child a week seemed like a small amount, but as I tried to do the same thing in my own life I realized how difficult even twenty minutes per child was in the midst of our hectic family schedule. But over the years, those small moments meant a lot in the creation of meaningful relationships with my family.

I want to reiterate that these practices have worked well for my family, and can be easily adapted to any family regardless of the size or makeup. Sister Linda K. Burton, when she was serving as the General Relief Society President, addressed the universal nature of family councils: "Because each family is unique in its composition, challenges, and strengths, family councils and the decisions they make will also be unique to each particular family. What might a family council look like for a family of young children? Because young children typically have very short attention spans, a family council might be as simple as asking a question and listening to a response during a brief moment of calm. At bedtime, the dinner table, or just before or after family prayer."[93]

What if you are a single parent? Elder M. Russell Ballard taught, "Single parents often come home tired after a day at work. Then they've got to prepare dinner and help children with homework. They stretch themselves emotionally to the point that they may not have the energy or time to sit down and have a family council in a formal way." But rather using these stresses to excuse family councils, Elder Ballard taught, "*But the more stress there is on a family, the more important family councils become.*"[94]

---

93 Linda K. Burton, "Sabbath Observance Through Family Councils," Ward Council Training Video, 2015.

94 "Family Councils: A Conversation with Elder and Sister Ballard," *Ensign* June 2003, emphasis added.

Rather than giving up on family councils because we are too stressed or pressed for time, we might need to change the way we look at family councils. Elder Ballard taught, "The key for a single parent—and other parents as well—is to take advantage of informal counseling opportunities with a child. They might be while driving in the car, doing the dishes, or in the morning and evening just before prayers. As tired as you may be, it's wise to invest the time and attention it takes to make an effective connection with your children. It is far better to lovingly communicate in the beginning, while they are young, than to try and hammer it into them later when behavior changes more slowly."[95]

Other family configurations can adapt as needed. Sister Burton taught, "What might a family council look for a newly wed couple or even an elderly couple? It could be as simple as a walk where the couple discusses concerns, goals, or makes plans that are unique to their family." She added, "Many Church members live alone. Who might they counsel with as a family of one? We can find the answer in Alma 37:37: 'Counsel with the Lord in all thy doings, and he shall direct thee for good.' Each family is unique and so are the needs."[96] Families come in all shapes, configurations, and sizes, but the principles of family councils are applicable to all.

## Storge: The Ground We Stand on and the Reason We Are Here

We have compared Eros to fire, Philia to water, and Storge to earth. As we mentioned, Storge is sometimes subject to seismic events, but it is among the most stable forces in our lives. We build all of the meaningful structures of our lives on its foundation. Its gravitational pull keeps us centered on what matters most in our lives and what brings us the greatest happiness. In the scriptural account of creation, Adam and Eve came forth, formed from the "dust of the ground" (Genesis 2:7), a phrase emphasizing their connection to each other and all things. The name "Adam" in Hebrew literally means "one from the soil," while the name Eve means "life."[97] The symbology is potent—Adam came from the earth, Eve came from Adam, and together they

95 "Family Councils: A Conversation with Elder and Sister Ballard," *Ensign* June 2003.

96 Linda K. Burton, "Sabbath Observance Through Family Councils," Ward Council Training Video, 2015.

97 "Eve meaning," *Abarim Publications,* https://www.abarim-publications.com/Meaning/Eve.html#.Xw3cNS2-m-o

form life. President Russell M. Nelson emphasized this connection when he taught, "Grand as it is, planet Earth is part of something even grander—that great plan of God. Simply summarized, the earth was created that families might be. Scripture explains that as husband and wife 'shall be one flesh, and all this that the earth might answer the ends of its creation.'"[98] It is indeed grand to think that the ground beneath our feet, the sky above our heads, and all that surrounds us exists to allow God to teach us how to love as a family. Storge really is the kind of love that makes the world go 'round.

98 Russell M. Nelson, "The Creation."

# Interlude: A Stranger in the Courts of the Holy Temple

Early one morning, Jesus of Nazareth walked to the Mount of Olives and then turned to ascend into one of the courts of the grand Temple of Herod. Wherever he went, crowds tended to follow, and soon a group of people gathered around Jesus, listening intently to His teachings. The record is silent on what the Savior taught the people that morning; instead it notes that His teaching was interrupted when a raucous group of scribes and Pharisees dragged a woman into the midst of the crowd, roughly tossing her at the feet of Jesus.

"Master, this woman was taken in adultery, in the very act," they declared, speaking more for the benefit of the gathered crowd than for the Savior. The accusers come across as less interested in the woman and her sins and more interested in presenting a moral quandary to the teacher from Galilee. "Now Moses in the law commanded us, that such should be stoned: but what sayest thou?" (John 8:5) The gauntlet was thrown down, and Jesus faced the dilemma of showing mercy to the woman and coming across as tolerant of a heinous sin or participating in a ritual murder and walking away with blood—even if it was the blood of the guilty—on his hands.

The law was clear, declaring that "the adulterer and the adulteress shall surely be put to death" (Leviticus 20:10). The Savior's adversaries likely reveled in the dilemma placed in front of Him, knowing that Jesus was fully acquainted with the law and knew the punishments for adultery. The people looked to Jesus as a merciful and profound teacher but also as someone who insisted on sincere adherence to the commandments. Both groups looked to the Savior for a response, waiting for Him to open his mouth and declare harsh justice or weak mercy. Was Jesus of Nazareth at last backed into a corner without any escape? It is easy to imagine the tension rising as all groups waited with anticipation for the Savior's response.

Instead of uttering words of consolation or the harsh tones of a thunderous condemnation, the teacher stooped down, silent, and began writing on the ground.

We do not know what Jesus wrote on the ground, or how long he forced the crowd or His adversaries to stand in awkward silence while he traced lines in the dirt with his finger. Eventually the anticipation overcame them and they again began to demand a reply. Jesus simply continued to trace lines on the ground with his finger, only heightening the tension of the situation. The crowd likely grew more boisterous as the seconds without a response ticked onward. Suddenly the Savior rose and declared simply, "He that is without sin among you, let him first cast a stone at her," then bent down again, and continued writing on the ground with his finger (John 8:7-8).

We imagine a silence falling over the crowd. Each stood stunned at the answer. Instead of yelling loudly about the sins of the woman dragged into the court, Jesus had turned their accusations around on them. Did they hear the sound of stones dropping to the ground as those who had come prepared to take a life reflected on their own transgressions and silently turned and walked out of the grounds of the holy house? Even those who came to the listen to the Savior rather than to accuse were convicted by their own transgressions and wandered out of the temple court. All the while, the Savior continued to trace figures on the ground. Finally, only Jesus and the condemned adulterer stood in the court.

He stood up, glanced around, and saw no one with them. He looked at the woman and casually remarked, "Woman, where are those thine accusers? hath no man condemned thee?" It is difficult to imagine the woman, who only moments before was violently dragged to the temple anticipating her own death, glancing up at the teacher and meekly saying, "No man, Lord." Jesus simply replied, "Neither do I condemn thee: go, and sin no more" (John 8:1–11).

This simple tale in the Gospel of John is remarkable for the economy of its storytelling. In just eleven verses it raises a number of profound questions about the nature of sin, forgiveness, judgment, and condemnation. It offers no easy answers for anyone who reads it, presenting one of the most complex paradoxes to any person who studies the scriptures. Does the Messiah not condemn the sin of adultery? Only a few verses later he declares, "Before Abraham was, I am," essentially declaring Himself to be the God of the Old Testament and the author of the law used to condemn the adulteress (John 8:58). He wrote the law! Why did He make an exception for this woman? Why show compassion?

It appears from the text that the Savior did not know the woman in question. She was neither friend, family, nor even acquaintance, yet he showed her love. This was not Philia, Eros, or Storge at work. Instead, a deeper love overrode the law and allowed the Savior to show love for a complete stranger when he had no compelling reason do so. With nothing to gain, the Savior showed love for a woman engaged in a serious sin and disarmed a bloodthirsty crowd with only a handful of spoken words. How could such power come from a single sentence?

Jesus drew on the most profound and most powerful of loves to disarm the crowd and save the woman from her accusers and from herself: a love unnatural to us but essential to our survival and happiness. It comes only as a gift from God to those who seek it. It is the kind of love that demands nothing from those to whom it is given to but rewards the giver with the most edifying effects of any type of love. It is the only love that never fails.

It is the highest and most Godlike of the loves, so different from the other loves that in scripture it often uses a separate word. It is Agape, or Charity.

# Agape

*"A man filled with the love of God, is not content with blessing his family alone, but ranges through the world, anxious to bless the whole of the human family."* —Joseph Smith Jr.

In his first letter to the Corinthians, the Apostle Paul included a lengthy discourse on the spiritual gifts given to the Saints. Spiritual gifts are supernatural abilities given to those worthy and in need of them—it is likely that if Paul were speaking in our world today, he would have called them spiritual superpowers. This list includes amazing gifts such as healing, miracles, prophesy, speaking in tongues, and interpreting tongues; it is an impressive collection of the powers beyond normal human capacity that God regularly grants to those who can use them to further His work. Paul teaches that each person is given different gifts, and the different gifts are used in different ways to bless the Church. He even urges members to "covet earnestly the best gifts" (1 Corinthians 12:31). What is the best gift? Paul suddenly shifts the conversation to answer that very question. "Though I speak with the tongues of men and of angels, and have not charity, I am become as sounding brass, or a tinkling cymbal." To Paul, everything else is noise, only charity matters. "And though I have the gift of prophecy, and understand all mysteries, and all knowledge; and though I have all faith, so that I could remove mountains, and have not charity, I am nothing." While the Apostle does not denigrate any of the spiritual gifts or knowledge he has already described, he points out their hollow nature without charity. "And though I bestow all my goods to feed the poor, and though I give my body to be burned, and have not charity, it profiteth me nothing" (1 Corinthians 13:1–3). Charity is the gift of gifts, the highest virtue for men and women to pursue, the attribute that gives meaning and substance to all Christlike acts. In his most profound discourse, Mormon taught, "Charity is the pure love of Christ, and it endureth forever, and whoso is found possessed of it at the last day it shall be well with him" (Moroni 7:47). And so, at last, we come to the greatest and most important of all the loves, charity, or in Greek, agape.

## What Is Agape?

In *The Four Loves*, C. S. Lewis describes Eros, Philia, and Storge as the "natural loves."[99] These loves are explainable by the natural circumstances surrounding us from the first moment we arrive in mortality. It is a biological drive to want to procreate, and Eros facilitates those drives. It is also natural to look after your family, especially children, since the continued transfer of your DNA to another generation leads to a biological immortality. Storge fills this need. Friendship is not just a nice thing to have, it is an essential for survival. We need other people to make our day-to-day existence possible. Without Philia we have a much poorer chance of survival in this world. But how does Agape fit into this picture? Does it fill a biological need to help a wounded stranger on the side of the road? Is there an evolutionary advantage found in demonstrating compassion toward your enemies? How does Christlike behavior help us get ahead in the world? In many ways, Agape is unnatural.

Lewis describes Agape as "divine energy," something fundamentally different from the natural loves. Playing off Paul's teaching that Agape "seeketh not her own" (1 Corinthians 13:5), Lewis writes, "This primal love is Gift-love. In God there is not hunger that needs to be filled, only plenteousness that desires to give."[100] We don't experience agape because there is something in it for us; we experience it out of a deep spiritual desire to give to others. In this way, Agape makes us like God, for what could we possibly give to God? Everything in the universe belongs to God. There is only one

99 Lewis, "The Four Loves," 116.

100 Lewis, 126.

thing we can give to God, or one thing that God really wants from us. As Elder Neal A. Maxwell taught, "The submission of one's will is really the only uniquely personal thing we have to place on God's altar. The many other things we 'give' are actually the things He has already given or loaned to us."[101] And the gift we give to God is really something He asks us to give by loving all the people around us. This teaching is found over and over again in sacred scripture. King Benjamin taught that "when ye are in the service of your fellow beings ye are only in the service of your God" (Mosiah 2:17). This love is completely separated from need and therefore is not natural, but supernatural. It is the love that makes us like God.

Agape is also one of the grand teachings separating Christ from all of the other profound teachers, philosophers, and religious leaders in the history of the world. Several decades ago, historian Michael H. Hart undertook the ambitious task of determining the one hundred greatest people that ever lived. On his final list, Jesus Christ ranked third, something surprising to both Christians and non-believers. The author noted that Jesus was profoundly impactful but wrote that "it was primarily as an ethical teacher that Jesus left his mark" and "it is surely pertinent to ask to what extent his ideas have influenced the world." One of Jesus's central teachings was the Golden Rule, expressed most plainly by the Savior when He said, "Therefore all things whatsoever ye would that men should do to you, do ye even so to them: for this is the law and the prophets" (Matthew 7:12). There is no doubt that the Golden Rule is widely accepted as a universal standard of morality. However, the historian argues, "the Golden Rule was an accepted precept in Judaism long before Jesus was born. Rabbi Hillel, the leading Jewish rabbi of the first century B.C., explicitly enunciated the Golden Rule and pronounced it the foremost principle of Judaism." He continues, "Nor was the notion known only to the Western world. The Chinese philosopher Confucius had proposed it in about 500 B.C., and the saying also appears in the *Mahabharata,* an ancient Hindu poem." He correctly points out, "The philosophy behind the Golden Rule is accepted by almost every major religious group."[102]

While Latter-day Saints see similarities in morality across cultures as a sign of God "manifesting himself unto all nations" (Book of Mormon Title

---

101 Neal A. Maxwell, "Swallowed Up in the Will of the Father," *Ensign,* November 1995, 22–24.

102 Michael H. Hart, *The 100: A Ranking of the Most Influential People in History* (New York: Hart Publishing, 1978), 20.

Page), Hart's assertions do raise the question, what original idea did Jesus contribute to the world pantheon of ethics and morality? There is a profound idea from the teachings of Christ that is radically different from anything taught by any other teacher in any other culture. In His most famous sermon, Jesus taught, "Ye have heard that it hath been said, Thou shalt love thy neighbor, and hate thine enemy," a standard restatement of the Golden Rule. Then comes the radical part: "But I say unto you, Love your enemies, bless them that curse you, do good to them that hate you, and pray for them which despitefully use you, and persecute you; That ye may be the children of your Father which is heaven." Jesus continues his argument, pointing out, "If ye love them which love you, what reward have ye? Do not even the publicans the same? And if ye salute your brethren only, what do ye more than others? do not even publicans so? Be ye therefore perfect, even as your Father which is in heaven is perfect" (Matthew 5:43–48).

The teaching of loving your enemies is a dramatic departure from anything taught in any religion on earth. It is natural and makes sense to love someone who loves you back, or at the very least, does you no harm. But loving your enemies is not natural. It is, however, the essence of agape. Agape seeks nothing from others, and at times it even means loving people when there is no reward, no recompense, and no sensible reason for doing so. Eros, Philia, and Storge come naturally to us, but Agape can only be experienced as a gift from the divine, as a connection between ourselves and something larger and more powerful. It is the metaphorical point where humanity and divinity touch and power from on high is placed into a mortal being.

## Agape and the Natural Loves

We can extend our metaphor about the elements and the four loves: if Eros is symbolized by fire, Philia by water, and Storge by earth, then perhaps the most fitting symbol for agape is air. It is an element in the other four loves, but it is also larger. Like the atmosphere that surrounds us, it is the most essential to our spiritual survival, yet the least obvious from our natural viewpoint. Like air, it is the most difficult of the loves for us to discern with our physical senses, but it permeates all things and is in all things. Agape provides meaning and longevity to the other loves, transforming them from transient, temporal feelings into aspects of the eternal worlds. Each of the three natural loves is transformed by the addition of agape.

As mentioned before, one of the Prophet Joseph Smith's most important teachings was his April 1843 statement that "that same sociality which exists among us here will exist among us there, only it will be coupled with eternal glory, which glory we do not now enjoy" (D&C 130:2).[103] While we have already considered this statement in the context of Storge, let's look at what it means for the other natural loves, along with Agape. In context, just before the Prophet shared this teaching he also taught, "When the Savior shall appear we shall see him as he is. We shall see that he is a man like ourselves" (D&C 130:1).[104] According to one of the Prophet's scribes, William Clayton, the reason why Joseph gave both of these teachings was to explain the teaching in the scriptures that "when he [the Savior] shall appear, we shall be like him, for we shall see him as he is" (1 John 3:2, Moroni 7:48). What is the key to coupling our social relationships with eternal glory? To become like Christ. What is the primary attribute possessed by Christ but lacking in natural men and women? "Charity is the pure love of Christ, and it endureth forever, and whoso is found possessed of it at the last day, it shall be well with him" (Moroni 7:47). The gateway to eternity, to making the other loves - Eros, Philia, and Storge - last into the eternities, is to become like Christ and to love like Christ loves.

Consider the strengths and flaws of Eros. Eros is the most exhilarating of the natural loves, but it is also the most unstable. It can raise us to the highest heights, but it exists on a very unstable foundation because it depends primarily on how the object of our Eros feels about us in response. It is also can be selfish, seeking constant approval and validation from the person we feel Eros for. How do we make Eros become more than just a quick burst of flame, one that produces a lot of light and heat but then is extinguished? It must be mixed with Agape. We must feel Christlike love for the person we are in romantic love with. Most people sense this need intuitively. Though Eros can be a very needy, self-centered love, most of us recognize the need for selflessness in our romantic relationships. When I have asked students in my classes, "How do you know if you are really, truly in love?" the most common answer has been, "When I put the needs of the other person ahead of my own." They can distinguish between a self-involved love

103 "Appendix 2: William Clayton, Journal Excerpt, 1–4 April 1843," p. 67, The Joseph Smith Papers, https://www.josephsmithpapers.org/paper-summary/appendix-2-william-clayton-journal-excerpt-1-4-april-1843/3

104 "Appendix 2: William Clayton, Journal Excerpt, 1–4 April 1843," p. 67.

affair—pure Eros—and the lasting unselfish love created when Eros and Agape are mingled together.

When we experience Eros, we generally rush to put our best self in front of the object of our affections. But all of us know that this version of self is an illusion. We can only present our best selves for so long before cracks in the portrait begin to appear. Physical beauty fades, our wit and words fail us, and eventually our charm will evaporate in the midst of an argument or a frustrating day. Those in Eros with each other spend usually spend significant amounts of time together, and that means eventually we will all be exposed as the flawed and imperfect beings we are. If we cannot feel Agape for the people we love romantically, our relationships are doomed to failure. While the intensity of the first feelings of Eros are wonderful, we need to develop agape for those we love too. We need to see them the way Christ does and love them not just for their good qualities but also for their weaknesses. While Eros accepts the best of us, Eros and Agape together create the warm glow of a love that accepts who we really are, for better or worse.

Philia is also strengthened when it is supplemented by Agape. Friendship is generally a more stable, less dramatic, and less demanding kind of love than Eros, but it does have tendencies toward selfishness and need. We have compared Philia to a refreshing flow of water. If we are constantly thinking of ourselves, or what we want and how our friends can help us get it, Philia tends to dry up like a stream cut off from its source. Just as nearly every water source on Earth is fed by the rain and snow from the atmosphere's precipitation, true Philia draws from Agape. Our friendships are most healthy when we see them not as avenues to get what we want but as a way to help and lift those around us. This focus does not mean that we never seek or accept help from our friends. Sometimes the best way for us to cultivate Philia with others is to seek and allow their help.

In my current occupation, I teach in a large department filled with dozens of very talented people. When I first arrived, my insecurities about being in such an elite group led me to think that I would make new friends if I could just show them how good I was at everything and how my talents could help them. I worked hard to show my competence, and I did succeed in impressing a few, but not many. It was when I opened up and asked for help from others that doors began to open. Philia mixed with Agape is a two-way street. It works best when we serve others and create an impulse in others to serve by being humble enough to accept help. If Philia is like water, then it continually flows downward. Those who are humble and don't seek to place themselves above others make friends the most easily. Philia, for all of it goodness, can still turn into something we seek to gain the praise of the world. We often tout our number of friendships, or brag about our high-profile connections in a way meant to inflate our own egos. In contrast, "[Agape] vaunteth not itself, is not puffed up, doth not behave itself unseemly, [and] seeketh not her own" (1 Corinthians 13:4–5). Our friendships hold the potential to be some of the most important relationships in our journey back to God, but only if we see our friends the way the Savior sees them.

Storge is perhaps the least selfish of the natural loves, but only because the selfishness manifests itself in different ways. We often go to great lengths to give of ourselves to our family members, and family is where we come closest to feeling unconditional love. Even before each of my children were born, I remember feeling that I would do anything for them. When I first saw them, I felt a surge of love and a desire to make them happy. Because of our natural connection to our family members, we feel a deep desire to make them happy and protect them from the ills of the world. It is easy to be deeply involved in their lives because Storge is so strong a force in our connections with other people.

But the desire to involve ourselves in the lives of our family members can also be twisted into a desire to control their lives and impede their right to make their own choices. President Russell M. Nelson once recalled a story illustrating this point from his own family. "When our youngest daughter was about four years of age, I came home from hospital duties quite late one evening. I found my dear wife to be very weary . . . so I offered to get our four-year-old ready for bed." President Nelson soon set about getting his young daughter ready for bed, but perhaps too directly. "I began to give the orders: 'Take off your clothes, hang them up; put on your pajamas; brush your teeth; say your prayers' and so on, commanding in a manner befitting a tough sergeant in the army." In the midst of this flurry of commands, President Nelson's daughter caught him off guard. "Suddenly she cocked her head to one side, looked at me with a wistful eye, and said, 'Daddy, do you own me?'" Years later he reflected on the powerful message given through a four-year-old: "She taught me an important lesson. . . . No, we don't own our children. Our parental privilege is to love them, to lead them, and to let them go."[105]

105 Russell M. Nelson, "Listen to Learn," *Ensign,* May 1991, 22.

The Apostle Paul taught that "charity seeketh not her own" (1 Corinthians 13:5). While Storge comes from a desire to help our family members, it can be subtly altered so that we are thinking not of what is best for them, but of what is best for us. We often use guilt and manipulation to force family members down the path we want them to travel rather than letting them find their own. One of the most difficult parts of feeling Storge for another person is learning to when to let go. We love them, and we feel we know what is best for them, but we must also respect the sacred principle of agency.

I often reflect on the example set by our Heavenly Parents during the Council in Heaven. We sometimes forget that the Satan and the "third part of the hosts of heaven" (Doctrine & Covenants 29:36) were also the sons and daughters of our Heavenly Parents. There is no doubt that it was painful for our Father and Mother in Heaven to see a portion of their children abandon the great plan of happiness. As omnipotent beings, they possessed the power to stop their wayward children from leaving. Why did they not intervene? The scriptures offer the answer: "because of their agency" (Doctrine & Covenants 29:36). Honoring agency is a part of Agape. At times the intense Storge we feel for our family tempts us to want to override their agency instead of allowing them to write their own story. When Agape is combined with Storge, we show love for those in our family by teaching correct principles and also by allowing them to govern themselves.

Another concern linked to Storge is the level of comfort we feel around our family members. Comfort around family is a positive sign, but it can also lead us to fail to extend the same courtesy to our family members that we would extend to complete strangers. At times I find myself treating the students in my classes with more kindness than my own family members. Elder Jeffrey R. Holland counseled, "Think of how many arguments could be avoided, how many hurt feelings could be spared, and, in a worst-case scenario, how many breakups and divorces could be avoided if we were not so easily provoked, if we thought no evil of one another, and if we not only did not rejoice in iniquity but didn't rejoice even in little mistakes." As Elder Holland alludes to here, "[Agape] is not easily provoked, thinketh no evil; rejoiceth not in iniquity, but rejoiceth in the truth" (1 Corinthians 13:5–6). A helping of Agape in our familial relationships eases the tension and makes our homes into places of validation and acceptance. Elder Holland continues, "Think the best of each other, especially of those you say you love. Assume the good and doubt the bad."[106]

All of the natural loves are strengthened when they are intermingled with Agape. Charity allows us to love complete strangers and the worst of enemies. Does it not make sense for it to also deepen our connections to our family members, friends, and romantic partners?

## How Do I Cultivate Agape?

Since Agape is a divine rather than a natural love, it comes as a spiritual gift from God. The scriptures offer a simple formula for obtaining charity. Mormon taught, "Wherefore my beloved brethren, pray unto the Father with all the energy of heart, that ye may be filled with this love [Agape], which he hath bestowed upon all who are true followers of his Son, Jesus Christ; that ye may become the sons of God" (Moroni 7:48). God does not hoard spiritual gifts. President George Q. Cannon taught, "If any of us are imperfect, it is our duty to pray for the gift that will make us perfect. Have I imperfections? I am full of them. What is my duty? To pray to God to give me the gifts that will correct these imperfections."[107] Charity is the universal cure for sin and weakness. It makes us more kind, enables us to cope with our trials, and helps us become like Christ. It is the gift we need the most to be a force for good. As President Cannon taught, "If I am an angry man, it is my duty to pray for charity, which suffereth long and is kind. Am I an envious man? It is my duty to seek for charity, which envieth not. So [it is] with all gifts of the Gospel."[108]

Once we have prayed for the gift to feel Agape for others, we need to start to apply it in our own lives. It is easier to feel Christlike love for others when we keep in mind this teaching of the Savior: "Inasmuch as ye have done it unto one of the least of these my brethren, ye have done it unto me" (Matthew 25:40). This greatly simplifies our world outlook. There are only two people on earth: you and the Savior. When we begin to learn see those around us, even our enemies, as people we have a sacred obligation to protect and nourish, agape begins to fill our hearts and minds. This does not mean that we compromise with wrong behavior; rather, agape is intended to compel us to love those around us for the sake of the Savior. President Dal-

106 Jeffrey R. Holland, "How Do I Love Thee?" BYU Speeches, 1999–2000, 160–61.

107 George Q. Cannon, *Millennial Star* 56 (April 23, 1864): 260–61.

108 Cannon, 260–61.

lin H. Oaks once outlined several possible reasons for why a person serves others. They range from the more selfish reasons such as hope for a personal reward or fear of punishment to purer reasons such as a sense of duty or hope of an eternal reward. The highest reason was charity, the pure love of Christ. "If our service is to be most efficacious," President Oaks taught, "it must be accomplished for the love of God and the love of his children."[109]

When I was a young teacher, an experience impressed this principle on my mind. I was teaching a class full of young, eager seminary students, with one exception. There was a young man in class who constantly showed up late, was disrespectful to me, and was cruel to the other students. I can handle a student with a bad attitude, but his comments to the other students, some of which left them devastated and in tears, really bothered me. I started to feel a sense of relief when this student missed class, and I felt my anger rising when he walked in the door. One day when he didn't show up to class, I was in the middle of teaching when the power in the entire building went out. In the midst of some awkward laughter from the students, I left the room to go and check the breaker box. When I got there, the young man I dreaded coming to class was coming out of the room where the breaker boxes were located. I immediately stopped him and asked him if he was the one who had turned off the power to the entire building. He made a half-hearted attempt at some excuse, but it was clear that I had him at last, red handed. Seething with anger, I turned the breakers back on and then dragged the student down to the principal's office. I brought him, informed the principal he was responsible for the power going out and then demanded this young man be kicked out of seminary altogether. Then I left to go back and teach my class.

A few minutes later, the young men ambled back into my class and sat down, starting up with his regular routines. I was practically apoplectic with rage, but I managed to finish the lesson and excuse the class. Afterwards, I stormed down to the principal's office to ask why this young man was not immediately ejected from the building. My principal, who was a thirty-year veteran of teaching young people, calmly asked me to sit down. I sat, but then I burst out in anger, yelling, "I just can't teach him! I can't feel love for him! I don't even like him!" Rather than responding in a harsh tone, my principal looked at me and said softly, "I know that. I know this

109 Dallin H. Oaks, "Why Do We Serve?" *Ensign*, October 1984, https://www.churchofjesuschrist.org/study/general-conference/1984/10/why-do-we-serve

young man is difficult to love or even to like. But can you accept that the Savior loved him enough to die for him? Can you love him just because the Savior loves him?" This struck me. I was thinking of my wounded pride, my standing before the other students and teachers, and not of the place this young man was coming from. His behavior was terrible, but so was mine. I labeled him an enemy and worked to avoid him. I was able to love the students who liked or loved me but felt no charity for this student.

Over the next few weeks I made a genuine attempt to show love toward this young man. I attended his sporting events; I tried to find opportunities to speak with him in the hallway and treat him with respect during the class. I prayed earnestly for the gift of charity toward him. All the while, the words of my principal rang in my head, "Can you accept that the Savior loved him enough to die for him?" I began to see the young man differently and realized how much of his cruelty and disrespect was a product of his own insecurities. Over time, the young man softened. I wish I could say we became fast friends, but we did develop enough of a relationship to finish the year on good terms. I saw more dramatic effects in the feelings of the entire class. The students had sensed my anger and bad feelings toward this young man. When they saw me making an earnest effort to try and reach out to him, the feelings of love and comfort in the class increased considerably, and it became much easier to teach with the Spirit. The students recognized the virtue in leaving the ninety and nine to try and help the one (Luke 15:1–6). Finally, my soul had been cankered by the anger I felt toward the young man. Just acknowledging the Savior's love for him helped me to love him too. The highest and holiest form of love is to find love for those who don't love us back and might even hate us.

## Interlude: The Broken Warrior

Badly wounded, and only able to walk with assistance, Mormon looked over the battlefield. Stretched before him in every direction was a scene of carnage unparalleled in the history of his people. Mormon was no stranger to death having fought and led the armies of his people since he was a teenager, but even his war-weary eyes had never beheld a scene resembling this vision of horror. The bodies of men, women, and children, killed in combat, lay heaped upon the landscape. Along the way, Mormon had lost nearly everyone close to him. His wife and all of his children were gone, save his son Moroni, who assisted him as he limped across the fields of slaughter. Throughout his life he had witnessed the terrible decline of his people into barbarism. He had seen atrocities committed by both sides in a never ending war between those who called themselves Nephites and those who called themselves Lamanites. Now his part in the war was drawing to a close, with only twenty-four of his soldiers still found alive in the aftermath of the great battle of Cumorah.

It is difficult to imagine the overwhelming mixture of feelings that came over Mormon as he limped to a higher vantage point to behold the battlefield below. His people were cut down without any regard of their humanity. The bodies of children lay among the adult men and women who died in the battle. The motivating factor on both sides was simple hatred, the kind of hatred which burns away and semblance of mercy or humanity and leaves behind an inhuman desire to murder and pillage. Looking on the scene below the simplest course for Mormon was to allow himself to wallow in the hatred and anger for those who murdered his people. But he also knew that his people fought out of hatred and spite. He had seen his own people commit unspeakable atrocities against their foes, carrying horrific acts of violence that Mormon knew at times became worse than murder. The conflict at Cumorah was a terrible scene of murderers fighting murderers, and sweeping any innocent children or adults along with in the maelstrom of hatred.

Mormon fought the urge to give into his hatred. He must have wanted to hate his enemies for the slaughter of his people. He must have wanted hate his people for allowing themselves to fall from grace and become an obscene band of murderers themselves. But Mormon was a disciple of Jesus Christ. Only a short time before he had engraved the words of his master into a record of golden plates, intended to tell the sad story of his people, but also to pass along the teachings that only a few hundred years earlier had created an idyllic society. The Savior hold to His disciples,"Behold it is written also, that thou shalt love thy neighbor and hate thine enemy; But behold I say unto you, love your enemies, bless them that curse you, do good to them that hate you, and pray for them who despitefully use you and persecute you" (3 Nephi 12:43-44).

Was it possible in the face of the carnage Mormon saw to still love the enemies who had killed his people. Was it possible to love his own people who had become so depraved, and committed so many atrocities? The teachings of Mormon's Savior challenged him to try. His mind may have drifted back to a sermon he gave to the remaining disciples of Jesus among his people. "Cleave unto charity, which is the greatest of all, for all things must fail—But charity is the pure love of Christ, and it endureth forever; and whoso is found possessed of it at the last day, it shall be well with him" (Moroni 7:46-47). The words of his old sermon rang in his mind and in his heart. "My beloved brethren, pray unto the Father with all the energy of heart, that ye may be filled with this love, which he hath bestowed upon all who are true followers of his Son, Jesus Christ" (Moroni 7:48).

With the memory of these teachings in his mind, Mormon used the final remains of his strength to write a letter to the very people who had just murdered everyone he had ever known. He wrote to the blood enemies of his people to remind them of their shared heritage and their identity as the children of God. "Know ye that ye are of the house of Israel. Know ye that ye must come unto repentance, or ye cannot be saved . . . Know ye that ye must come to the knowledge of your fathers, and repent of all your sins and iniquities, and believe in Jesus Christ" (Mormon 7:2-3,5).

He didn't write out of malice. He wasn't seeking revenge. As he continued to write the hatred he felt over the murder of his people melted away in concern for the eternal welfare of the very people he had spent his life fighting. In his last moments on earth, he found the strength in his broken and battered body to write a letter of love, an epistle of charity, to his worst enemies. Mormon lived in the darkest of times, but he refused to allow darkness to extinguish the light of Christ that burned in his own heart. He spent his final moments composing a message of consolation and forgiveness to the people who killed his family.

Eventually Mormon's own life was taken. No details are provided about his last moments on earth, but his son, Moroni, briefly mentions that he was slain. A man of peace, forced to spend almost his entire life in the midst of the worst of violence, at last fell victim to it as well. But as the last breath left Mormon's body, he knew his words would live on. His last surviving child picked up the record carrying it to a safe place and adding his own witness along the way. Mormon's final act of love - of charity - was to transform the story of his grief and loss into a book filled with promises of love and redemption.

## Loving Our Enemies

So far we have only been discussing love with people who love us back. It is easy and natural to love the people we feel Eros, Philia, and Storge. It is the most natural thing in the world to love people who love us. But with Agape, Jesus asked us to do something that isn't natural, that may even be supernatural. In the sermon on mount the Savior taught, "Love your enemies, bless them that curse you, do good to them that hate you, and pray for them which despitefully use you, and persecute you; That ye may be the children of your Father which is in heaven" (Matthew 5:44-45). This is perhaps the most radical teaching of Jesus Christ, and the final step on our journey to become like God.

To our natural sensibilities, the idea of loving people who hate us and despitefully use us might seem nonsensical. But, let's add a few clarifications. Loving your enemies does not mean that we ignore injustice, tolerate every type of behavior, or let ourselves be taken advantage of by immoral people. It means that we find a way to love our enemies in spite of what they do to us. The Savior was fearless in pointing out the wickedness and cruelty of his enemies, but he was also able to forgive them. When he was being nailed to the cross, Jesus uttered one of the most moving statements of His entire ministry, pleading, "Father, forgive them; for they know not what they do" (Luke 23:34). There is debate over whom the Savior was forgiving those words, but regardless of whether it was the soldiers carrying out the act, or the leaders who condemned Him to death, the statement is no less powerful or moving. In any scenario, Jesus was offering forgiveness towards those responsible for His death. This is one of the greatest acts of Agape ever recorded.

We can still see remarkable acts of forgiveness and reconciliation in the world around us. Like most of you, I was shocked, angry and hurt when I witnessed the terror attacks on the United States on September 11, 2001. I was in the middle of teaching a high school seminary class when a tardy student informed the class of an accident in New York City. So many of my students began chattering about the event that I agreed to stop the lesson and go check the television in the faculty room (this was before cell phones and instantaneous news updates). I walked in to see all of the other teachers in the building glued to the screen, watching the events unfold at the World Trade Center. I stared in disbelief for a few moments. When the second plane hit the buildings, we all suddenly knew this wasn't an accident, but a terrible act of violence on innocent civilians.

I spent the rest of the day sorting through my feelings, trying to stay strong and confident for my students, and listening as they ran the gamut of emotions. Some of them began talking about how their lives might change because of the attacks. A few expressed a desire to find the people responsible for the attacks and hurt them for what they did. I came home that day, and sat glued to the screen, my heart filled with righteous anger.

In the days following the attacks I heard my students and colleagues make some very direct statements about the people who attacked our country and our desire for revenge. Outside of the immediate context following the attacks, these remarks might seem terribly bigoted toward my brothers and sisters who practice Islam or come from Arabic countries. But there were a lot of raw emotions in the wake of the attacks, and I have to admit to feeling a little confused and angry myself. Still, it made it challenging to teach the gospel of Jesus Christ when my students continuously called for payback for the attacks on our country.

In the midst of these tumultuous events, I remember seeing that President Gordon B. Hinckley was going to appear on the cable news show *Larry King Live.* The host of the show, Larry King, was not a Latter-day Saint but his wife was, and in the wake of the attacks, I think he invited President Hinckley on his program to gain a spiritual perspective on the attacks. I can remember vividly that during the interview, the screen was split into two parts. One part showed President Hinckley calmly testifying and answering questions, while the other part of the screen showed workers still sifting through the smoldering remains of the World Trade Center. President Hinckley testified of his certainty about life after death, and his faith in the plan and mercy of God, despite the horrible nature of the attacks.

After a few remarks, the lines were opened for callers. One of the first questions given to President Hinckley was, "I'd like to ask President Hinckley, as a man of God, how he feels about these men that committed these atrocities against us?" President Hinckley responded, "Well, I feel terrible about them. I just think that they have done the worst kind of thing that anyone can conceive of. It is a terrible thing which they've done and they will stand before the bar of God and be judged by him." Larry King then asked, "Do you forgive them?" President Hinckley's reply showed his love for both the victims of the attacks and the people who carried them out. "I don't carry in my heart malice toward anyone. I believe that justice must prevail. If there has been wickedness or if there has been evil, we will pay for it . . . And I think those who have committed this atrocity will have to pay for it." He paused, and then continued, "But in my own heart, I tried to cultivate a spirit of Christian love without bitter malice or unkindness, but only love concerning those who have suffered so much . . . I have an absolutely solid faith concerning the eternity of life, concerning the fact that we're all sons and daughters of God, regardless of our religious persuasion, regardless of our nationality. We're sons and daughters of God. He expects good things of us."[110]

Those words resonated with me. President Hinckley saw no conflict between bringing the terrorists to justice, and also seeing them as his brothers, fellow sons of God. His words formed a marked contrast to the images of destruction and sorrow shown on the other side of the screen. But like Jesus Christ, he found the power to forgive. As a true witness of Christ, President Hinckley knew that he had to forgive. The teachings of his Master showed him that failing to forgive would only deepen the wounds in himself and his country that he was trying to bind up.

Now, I am not saying this type of forgiveness is easy or comes naturally to us. Mormon admonishes us to pray with all the energy in our hearts precisely because it is not natural. It is a gift from God, a divine superpower allowing us to forgive and love beyond our regular capacity. For most of us this capacity grows within us as we seek to serve and honor God. But like other spiritual gifts, it can come in an instant if there is a need.

I once met a man who experienced an instantaneous infusion of Agape. Frank Day grew up on a farm in Utah. He lived a quiet life assisting his father on the farm, until the attack on Pearl Harbor on December 7, 1941. In the aftermath of the attacks, Frank enrolled in the Marines and spent the next four years serving in South Pacific, fighting in some of the most horrific combat of the Second World War. His training as a Marine taught him

110 CNN Larry King Live Transcript, September 14, 2001, http://edition.cnn.com/TRANSCRIPTS/0109/14/lkl.00.html, accessed December 15, 2022.

to dehumanize the enemy, and his experiences pushed him further to hate the Japanese soldiers he fought during the bloody campaigns of the Pacific War.

When the war ended Frank returned home and began a career as a seminary teacher. He was gifted with a love for young people and for the scriptures, and he enjoyed every minute of his work. After several years in the classroom he was appointed to serve as an administrator in the Church Educational System. He joined the leadership of Church Education at a time when the worldwide expansion of the Church was accelerating. As area assignments were given by administrators, he was filled with anxiety. He later recalled, "I didn't want [Asia], and yet I had the feeling that was the area I would and should be assigned to. I had been in [Asia] in the military as a Marine and I had been trained that the enemy was the Japanese. The Marines trained well - not only how to use weapons, but how to hate the enemy."[111]

Frank soon found himself on a plane to Okinawa to meet with the local mission president who was Japanese. In a strange twist of fate, Okinawa was the last place Frank fought during the Pacific War, and he hadn't been back since then. The last time he set foot on Okinawa it was a bloody battlefield, with heavy casualties on both sides, and Kamikaze planes streaking overhead in a desperate attempt to beat back the American invasion. He later remembered, "When that airplane landed, I wondered what I would say and how I would respond. I had a strong urge to stay on the airplane . . . I wondered how I could talk about the teachings of Jesus, the mission of Joseph Smith, love, service, and all the other teachings of the gospel with people I had learned to hate."[112] He went through customs and saw the mission president waiting for him.

What happened next changed Frank's life. "As I took two or three steps toward the mission president, the Japanese brother, it was one of the most unusual experience I think I'll ever have. In a matter of seconds, the bitterness and the hatred, the training and the fear of years, was suddenly eliminated. I stepped up and it was the most natural things in the world to put my arms around Brother Kan Watanabe, the mission president. He put his arms around me and all of the hatred was gone and the love the [peo-

---

111 Frank Day Oral History, interviewed by David J. Whitaker, July 22, 1977, Church History Library, Salt Lake City, OH 366, 16.

112 Day Oral History, 17.

ple] was instilled in me at that time . . . Since that day the only answer I can give to anyone is that the Lord stepped in to assist and the enmity was taken away, completely wiped out, and have a great love for the [Asian people], the Japanese as much as any of them."[113]

What Frank Day experienced in the Okinawa airport is exactly why Mormon describes Agape as a spiritual gift. What happened that day was not normal. The training, anger, and hatred of one of the most savage wars in history cannot be overcome in a moment by any means of mortal men and women. But God has the capacity the reach a person's heart and heal them of the emotional and spiritual damage they have suffered. We talk at length about the Savior's power to heal physical maladies, but His greater power lies in healing the unseen wounds we all carry with us.

I experienced something similar to Frank Day, though not quite as dramatic. I was in charge of a historical conference a few years ago. The conference drew in all kinds of historians, some of whom were very hostile towards the Church. One in particular had been making the rounds making outrageous charges about the Book of Mormon, Joseph Smith, and some of the members of our faith. Every time I saw this individual I was tempted to walk up and give him a piece of my mind. I saw his statements not just as misguided but as malicious, intended to stir up hatred against the Church of Jesus Christ and its members.

At a banquet near the end of the conference I was running around seeing to the needs of the attendees. I was scrambling so much that once the actual dinner began, the only empty seat was next to this person. I had no desire to sit down next to him, worrying that I might lose my cool and make an awkward scene. I briefly thought about just standing in the back of the room and waiting things out. But someone else at the table beckoned for me to come over, and I found myself seated next to this person who had said terrible things about some of the dearest teachings of my faith. I hesitated at first, but then the thought "Love your enemies, do good to them who despitefully use you" flashed into my mind. I decided that I needed to really put that teaching to the test, and I sat down.

I can't say that this person became my best friend, but we did have a pleasant conversation and I learned a lot about his life and background. We talked back and forth for over an hour and my anger was abated. I still disagree with some of the things he says and does, but I also came to see him

113 Day Oral History, 18.

as my brother. We have different goals and different motivations, but I can honestly say that I came to love him in a Christlike way. I can have a fiery temperament at times, but during the dinner I found myself filled with the love of God. I can only account this to a spiritual gift from God. I didn't just tolerate this person, I felt like I learned to love him. Though I still have a long way to go when it comes to truly learning the meaning of Agape, it was a small step on my long journey of seeking to be like Christ.

## The Love that Never Faileth

In a letter to the Quorum of the Twelve, Joseph Smith taught, "Love is one of the leading characteristics of Deity, and ought to be manifested by those who aspire to be the Sons of God. A man filled with the love of God, is not content with blessing his family alone, but ranges through the world, anxious to bless the whole of the human family."[114] Agape is the love of God, a divine power, made manifest in his sons and daughters. Eros, Philia, and Storge are natural loves, and natural things eventually decay and perish unless they are mingled with divine power. Agape allows all of the wonderful loves we feel in this life to take on eternal life and exist with us in the eternities. If God expects us to master every form of love as part of our sojourn here on earth, Agape must be the foundation the other loves are built upon to become lasting, for "charity never faileth" (1 Corinthians 13:8). We can love our family, our friends, and our romantic partners in our own imperfect way, but Christ can take our loves, infuse them with agape and transform them into the kind of love that "endureth forever; and whoso is found possessed of it at the last day, it shall be well with him" (Moroni 7:47). We can even learn to love our most bitter enemies and avoid the damage that comes when we hold on to grudges and hatred. Agape gives us not only the power to survive in the this world, but to thrive and transcend the natural world around us. Agape makes the world go 'round.

---

114 "Letter to Quorum of the Twelve, 15 December 1840," p. 2, The Joseph Smith Papers, https://www.josephsmithpapers.org/paper-summary/letter-to-quorum-of-the-twelve-15-december-1840/2

# Interlude: A Scriptural Love Story

The Book of Ruth is an anomaly in the Old Testament. It is found in between the Book of Judges, arguable the most bloody and visceral book in the scriptural canon, and 1 Samuel, an epic story of the rise and fall of the first king of Israel. Compared to these two soaring narratives, the Book of Ruth is very low-key. There are no violent deaths, no dramatic twists in the plot, and no real villains. The story of Ruth takes place mostly in a tiny village, Bethlehem, in a time of peace. Everyone in the story is basically a good person. Orpah, the daughter-in-law who leaves Naomi at the beginning of the book, is not depicted as selfish, just not quite as devoted as Ruth. Likewise, the unnamed kinsman who rejects Ruth at the end of the book could have been depicted as the villain, but he is just acting out of a desire to protect his inheritance. The stakes are low. There are no empires or kingdoms in danger of destruction because of the actions of the heroes of the book. In some ways, the Book of Ruth is more like an old-fashioned romantic comedy than a biblical narrative. The book lacks any profound doctrinal statements about the nature of God but is rather content to show the gentle hand of God in the lives of its characters. In its consideration of their motives and its depictions of the actions, it exemplifies the kind of loves every virtuous person should strive to demonstrate.

The book of opens with a scene of tragedy. Naomi and husband Elimelech move to the country of Moab because of a famine. The Moabites are generally depicted as enemies of the Israelites in the Old Testament, and moving to their country underlines the desperate times experienced by Naomi and Elimelech. While the family sojourned in Moab, Elimelech passes, and the sons of Naomi—Mahlon and Chilion—marry two Moabite women, Orpah and Ruth. After another ten years, Mahlon and Chilion die also, and Naomi, Ruth, and Orpah are all left as childless widows. Naomi exhorts her daughters-in-law to return home, saying, "Go, return each to her mother's house: the Lord deal kindly with you, as ye have dealt with the dead, and with me" (Ruth 1:8). Regretfully, Orpah follows Naomi's counsel and returns home. Ruth, however, decides to stay. When Naomi requests one more time that Ruth go back to her family, Ruth gives one of the most moving speeches in all of biblical literature, declaring, "Entreat me not to leave thee, or to return from following after thee: for whither thou goest, I will go, and where thou lodgest, I will lodge: thy people shall be my people, and thy God my God. Where thou diest, will I die and there will I be buried: the Lord do so to me, and more also, if ought but death part thee and me" (Ruth 1:16–17). Seeing Ruth's determination, Naomi relents and the two women return to Israel, specifically to Naomi's home village of Bethlehem.

Their arrival in Bethlehem is not a happy scene. At the time, the village was a small settlement, consisting only of a few hundred people. When the arrival of the Ruth and Naomi creates as stir, Naomi makes a sad declaration to the people of her village. Instead of calling her Naomi (a Hebrew which means "sweet"), she says they should call her Mara (a word meaning "bitter") for, she declares, "the Almighty hath dealt very bitterly with me" (Ruth 1:20). Without much to hope for, and little property, wealth, or means, Naomi and Ruth settle into a life of poverty in the tiny town. The experience must have been especially bitter for Ruth, who gave up her family, her homeland, and her gods to live an impoverished life in Israel.

Rather than bemoaning her fate, Ruth sets out to provide for herself and Naomi. She goes out to the fields surrounding the town to find food. At the time, the Israelites permitted the practice of gleaning, in which the disadvantaged were allowed to pick up any sheaves of grain left on the ground after the crop was harvested. She was hard at work when she attracted the attention of Boaz, described as a "mighty man of wealth" (Ruth 2:1) and the owner of the field where Ruth labored. Boaz asks his servant who Ruth is and is told she is the Moabite who accompanied Naomi on her return. When Boaz introduces himself to Ruth in person, she is immediately overcome and falls on her face. As a foreigner, Ruth feels she has no right to expect favors from the Israelites. In response, Boaz offers to have his servants help her with her work and offers her food and drink. Rather than berating her as a foreigner or enemy of his people, Boaz instead acknowledges her sacrifices, telling Ruth, "It hath been fully shewed me, all that thou hast done unto thy mother in law since the death of thine husband: and how thou has left thy father and thy mother, and the land of thy nativity, and art come unto a people which thou knewest not heretofore." He then offered this blessing: "The Lord recompense thy work, and a full reward be given thee of the Lord God of Israel, under whose wings thou art come to trust" (Ruth 2:11–12). That day, Ruth came home with a full helping of grain and extra food to share with Naomi.

At this point, the story begins to shift from a tragedy to a comedy. When Ruth arrives home and describes her encounter with Boaz, Naomi must have practically leapt into the air with excitement. Boaz is a relative of Naomi's deceased husband and perhaps the solution to all of the problems facing the two women. Israelite custom allowed for a Levirate marriage, in which the woman of a deceased man invoked the law in order to compel the nearest living male relative of her deceased husband to marry her in the hopes of producing offspring. Boaz was related to Ruth's deceased husband, was well off, and was a prime candidate for a Levirate marriage that could lift the two women out of their impoverished state. In a scene that might not be out of place in a modern romantic comedy, Naomi urged Ruth to "wash thyself therefore, and anoint thee, and get thee down to the [threshing] floor" (Ruth 3:3). Not only did Naomi urge Ruth to present her best self, but she also told Ruth to wait until Boaz was finished eating and drinking—a moment of maximum happiness and comfort—before she made her approach. She should then wait until he laid down and uncover his feet, and then he would "tell thee what thou shalt do" (Ruth 3:4).

Ruth was likely flummoxed by this sudden information dump of Israelite custom, and she was probably overwhelmed at the notion of demanding marriage from a man she had only met that day. Naomi was well meaning, but she was also placing Ruth in a very vulnerable position. Nevertheless, she followed Naomi's directions, washed and anointed herself, and "did according to all that her mother in law bade her" (Ruth 3:6). Worse yet, when she arrived at the threshing floor where Boaz was staying for the night, he was already asleep. No doubt overwhelmed by the entire situation and unsure of what to do next, Ruth uncovered Boaz's feet without waking him, and then decided to lie down too. After midnight, Boaz woke up and found a woman unexpectedly lying at his feet. Startled, he blurted out "Who art thou?" Ruth, who was equally startled, stood her ground and declared her request for a Levirate marriage: "I am Ruth thine handmaid: spread therefore thy skirt over thine handmaid; for thou art a near kinsman" (Ruth 3:9).

Imagine the vulnerability Ruth showed in that moment. She was a foreigner, a young woman with no money and little means, and she had only a beginner's understanding of the Israelites and their customs. Other than the kindness he had showed her earlier in the day, she knew nothing about Boaz. Fortunately, Boaz was not the sort of person to take advantage of a young woman in a dangerous situation. He replied tenderly, "Blessed be thou of the Lord, my daughter, for thou hast shewed more kindness in the latter end than at the beginning, inasmuch as thou followedst not young men, whether poor or rich" (Ruth 3:10). Ruth's kindness and goodness had already won him over. He continued, "Fear not, I will do to thee all that thou requirest: for all of my people doth know that thou art a virtuous woman" (Ruth 3:11). Ruth entered Bethlehem a foreigner, but her kindness, goodness, and virtue had already endeared her to Boaz and the other people in the community. Ruth was not an Israelite by birth, but her actions showed her to be a person after God's own heart.

In just a moment, the story of Ruth completely reversed itself. Boaz also showed himself to also be a Christlike friend, someone who would do anything to help her. In her new homeland, Ruth had found family, friendship, security, and love. But any student of romantic comedies knows that there is always a complication to keep things from becoming too easy for the heroes. Immediately after pledging his help to Ruth, Boaz, as an honorable man, is also forced to explain why he could not marry her. "And now it is true that I am thy near kinsman: howbeit there is a kinsman nearer than I" (Ruth 3:12). It is implied in the story that Boaz wanted to marry Ruth, but because she invoked the law of Levirate marriage, he was forced to direct her to the nearest male relative.

Even when it seemed that Boaz was not fated to be Ruth's husband, he still protects her. Worried about what it would look like to see her sneaking out of the building in the middle of the night, he counsels Ruth to stay inside and rest. Beyond protecting her reputation, he also gives Ruth six shares of barley to take home so that she and Naomi would not go hungry. Finally, he offers to seek out the nearest kinsman, inform him of Ruth's request of marriage, and bring him to meet with her. Ever her protector, he then allows Ruth to return to Naomi's company, promising to visit her soon (Ruth 3:13–18).

The next day, Boaz meets the nearer kinsman (who is never given a name in the story) at the gate of the city. He quickly gathers together a council of elders from the city to witness the negotiation. Boaz opens the council with no mention of Ruth. Instead he tells the kinsman of a parcel of land belonging to Naomi's husband, Elimelech, and asks him if he would like to purchase it, using the biblical term "to redeem it" (Ruth 4:4). The kinsman jumps at the chance, offering to take the land. After seeing his eagerness to accept the property, Boaz then introduces the catch: "What day thou buyest the field of the hand of Naomi, thou must buy it also of Ruth the Moabitess, the wife of the dead, to raise up the name of the dead upon his inheritance" (Ruth 4:5). Hearing the full proposal, the kinsman balks, protesting, "I cannot redeem it myself, lest I mar mine own inheritance" (Ruth 4:6). Seeing his reluctance, Boaz immediately swoops in and offers to take responsibility for the field and to take Ruth as his wife. As was the custom of the time, he plucks off his shoe and gives it to his neighbor as a witness to seal the deal (this action was apparently the equivalent of a business handshake in ancient Israel). Boaz then proudly announces his intention for Ruth "to be my wife, to raise up the name of the dead upon his inheritance" (Ruth 4:10).

The people of the village join Ruth and Boaz in their rejoicing. The elders present as witnesses join in giving a Ruth a blessing, saying, "The Lord make the woman that is come into thine house like Rachel and like Leah, which two did build the house of Israel" (Ruth 4:11). To go from being the object of curiosity and derision to being compared to the founding matriarchs of the house of Israel is a feat never duplicated by any woman mentioned in the scriptures. Ruth and Boaz married, and soon after Ruth had a child named Obed. This story, filled with the small details of ordinary life, might have never been recorded if not for the fact that Ruth and Boaz's child, Obed, became the father of Jesse, who was in turn the father of David, the chosen king of united Israel (Ruth 4:17). David was the ancestor of Jesus Christ, and Ruth became one of only three women mentioned by name in the lineage of Jesus given in the New Testament (Matthew 1:5). And so Ruth, at first a stranger among the Israelites, became one of their princesses and the ancestor of the most important person ever born.

While story of Ruth is among the most simple and beautiful found in the scriptures, it also raises the question: what kind of love story is this? At first it is a story of Philia: the touching tale of two female friends, Ruth and Naomi, who cling to each other in the midst of overwhelming challenges. In the first chapter of the book, Naomi directly abandons any concept of a familial connection in her attempts to persuade Ruth to return to her own family. Then it becomes a story of Storge, in which Naomi schemes to take advantage of her family ties to Boaz in order to lift her and Ruth out of their life of poverty. Boaz too is compelled by his Storge to fulfill his family obligations and find a way for Ruth and Naomi to have their needs met. It is also undoubtedly a story of Eros, as Ruth and Boaz discover their mutual attraction for each other, marry, and have a child together. Last but not least, the entire story is a tale of Agape—of charity and Christlike love. Over and over again, the heroes of the story are given the opportunity to act selfishly. Ruth could have returned to her family and sought a new husband among her people. Boaz could have ignored Ruth in the field, seeing her just as another beggar looking for a free meal. Boaz also could have taken advantage of Ruth when she offered herself to him or embarrassed her in front of the village. The heroes in the story always chose a Christlike path when a choice was presented to them. The language becomes especially poignant when Boaz offers to redeem Ruth, giving her a home, a heritage, and an eternal family.

Many of our modern love stories focus solely on Eros. The Book of Ruth takes a more holistic approach, showing how Ruth and Boaz exemplify the best virtues of each of the four loves, especially Christlike love. Indeed, Boaz directly tells Ruth that it is her virtue and unselfishness that leads him to protect, help, and finally fall in love with her. In this story, as in all true love stories, Agape conquers all.

# The Four Loves in Everyday Life

*"Love is the defining characteristic of a disciple of Christ."*
*—Dieter F. Uchtdorf*

Our discussion began with a simple acknowledgment that the phrase "I love you" can mean a lot of different things. Increasing our understanding about the different kinds of love and the way we love others can help us lead happier and more productive lives and draw us closer to our Heavenly Parents and Jesus Christ. Elder Joseph B. Wirthlin taught, "Love is the greatest of all the commandments—all others hang upon it. It is our focus as followers of the Living Christ. It is the one trait that, if developed, will most improve our lives."[115] Learning about love and how to properly express it is nothing more or less than the art of learning to be like our Savior.

While I hope this discussion is helpful for you, I am under no illusion that you have not already experienced these different kinds of love in your own life. Loving others comes so naturally to us that it is practically like breathing. Despite all of the hatred, rancor, and contention we see in the

115 Joseph B. Wirthlin, "The Great Commandment," October 2007 General Conference.

world around us, most of our experiences with our brothers and sisters here on earth are loving. The four loves of Eros, Philia, Storge, and Agape are as visible in our everyday lives as the elements of fire, water, earth, and air that we have used as our metaphors throughout our discussion. Despite their commonness, there is great value in the study of each of these elemental parts of our mortal experience. The more deliberate we can be in recognizing and cultivating these different kinds of love, the more thoughtful and caring we will be toward our family, friends, and romantic partners.

## The Four Loves and a Single Person

While we have spent a considerable amount of time separating out and scrutinizing each of the four loves, we must also recognize that these loves are not separate from each other. Eros, Philia, and Storge overlap to a large degree, and Agape encompasses them all. Hopefully our family members become our close friends and our friends feel like family. It is an old cliché that friendship often turns into Eros over time. Most of the time, the feelings we have toward someone close to us is a mixture of all the loves, though recognizing the different forms of love is still helpful in our relationships. For instance, a couple might be good parents, and feel close as friends, but need to rekindle their Eros for each other. On rare occasions, I have also met couples who feel a strong Eros for each other but need to work on their friendship and infuse other parts of their relationship with more Christlike love.

Often, multiple loves are centered on the same person. I met my wife when we both worked on a maintenance crew for a theater during the summer after I arrived home from serving a mission. As we worked together over several months, we became friends, though our association was mostly through work. We fell into Philia with each other. I appreciated her sweetness and kindness, but I never thought of her as a romantic prospect, mostly because I was trying to wrap up a few romantic loose ends from before my time as a missionary. The catalyst that changed our relationship came when another member of the crew asked if I had ever considered asking her out. I replied, "I haven't thought about it. I guess I sort of think of her like a little sister." He expressed surprise and then said, "That's strange, because almost everyone on our crew has had a crush on her and asked her out, though no one has been able to get her to commit." He explained that she was always kind and polite on their dates, and everyone wanted to go out again, but she gently avoided entering into a serious relationship. I was intrigued. "You mean no one has been able to get her to commit to a relationship, or even a second date?" "Yeah, no one." Suddenly I was intrigued. Could I be the person to at last win the coveted second date? Challenge accepted.

I asked her out and she accepted. I then jumped into preparations for our date. One of my old tricks was to learn the meaning of a person's name as a conversation starter on a date. On our date I wrote out her name on a napkin and then told her its meaning in Hebrew was "God is my oath." I had also worked out a few other tricks to make the date lively, but I abandoned most of them as the date progressed. Talking to her was easy. She worked to make me comfortable as well, and I found myself moving from Philia into Eros. I won my coveted second date, and we moved into an exclusive relationship. Things moved forward pretty smoothly. The biggest challenge we faced in the early stages of our courtship was that all of the men on our maintenance crew threatened me with physical harm if I did anything to hurt her. I told them she was just as much a princess to me as she was to them. I also started a different job, just for my own safety.

One year after we met, we were sealed in the temple and moved into a tiny apartment. We spent the first two years of our marriage constantly moving from one small living space to another. We owned two or three items of furniture, and most of the apartments we lived in had no air conditioning or any of the nice refinements. We didn't care. We were in deep Eros with each and just being together was intoxicating. One day I came home and my wife gave me a small wrapped present. Inside was a small hooded sweatshirt. I asked her why she had bought a sweatshirt for her teddy bear and given it to me, and she kindly explained that it wasn't for the teddy bear, but for another member of our family. After a few more minutes of blunt explanation I realized what she was talking about: we were going to have a baby!

Nearly every parent can recall with great clarity the moment their child was born. My wife had a difficult labor that resulted in an emergency C-section. It was scary and distressing, but I remember all of that melting away when I saw the baby and held her in my arms. I felt a surge of love unlike anything I had previously experienced. I also looked over at my wife, exhausted from the labor and the surgery, and realized our relationship had entered a new stage. We had grown from Philia, to Eros, and now we were in deep Storge. She wasn't just my girlfriend, or even my wife anymore. Now she was the mother of my child.

Other children came to our family, and we found our love multiplied. Love does not exist in finite supply, and we found that every new child who joined our family resulted in an increase in love with abundance. Still, our marriage wasn't perfect. There were (and still are) misunderstandings, misfortune, and mistakes. Along the way, we had fights over trivial things, important things, or things I thought were trivial that turned out to be important. One of the most serious fights early on in our marriage happened because we held different opinions over which sister was "sense" and which was "sensibility" while watching the movie *Sense and Sensibility.* By the end of the night, we had called every English major we knew, and our parents wondered if our marriage was going to survive another Jane Austen adaptation. I haven't been a perfect husband. And my spouse, as wonderful as she is, hasn't been a perfect wife. There are days when everyone is tired or stressed, and we don't feel like we are in Eros with each other. There are times when some misunderstanding has led us to feel like we are not in Philia with each other. Fortunately, we have never had a day where our Storge was in danger of dissolution, though we have experienced many moments when couples we know and love have struggled through the end of their marriages. What gets us through the tough moments, when romance, friendship, and even family seem on the verge of fracture? Agape.

Agape—the gift of charity from God—allows us to love our worst enemies. As daunting as that sounds, it also gives us the grace to love our family, friends, and romantic partners. Eventually, every effort we make to project an image of perfection fails, and we are left with the harsh reality that "all are fallen, all are lost, and must perish except it be through the atonement" (Alma 34:9). Eros is undone by a jealously, a harsh word, or fading youth. Philia, though more stable, is undone by cruel acts, backbiting, or even something as simple as distance. The undoing of Storge is one of the great tragedies of our time, as we witness the fulfillment of warnings "that the disintegration of the family will bring upon individuals, communities, and nations the calamities foretold by ancient and modern prophets."[116] Christlike love provides the oxygen to keep the fires of Eros burning, is a chemical component of friendship, and infuses the bonds of family with strength. Agape, the love of Christ, is the unfailing force God sends to heal our relationships in romance, friendship, and family.

116 *The Family: A Proclamation to the World*, paragraph 8.

While it is useful to separate out the four loves in order to better understand them, we often witness the fusion of them in one person. My wife grew from being my friend, to the object of my Eros, to the center of my Storge. All along the way the Agape I feel for her, and certainly the Christ-like love she shows and bestows upon me, has kept every aspect of our love from destruction. The Savior's grace, manifested through the love of a righteous spouse, invigorates and strengthens all of the loves in our lives. The four loves cannot just overlap, but rather they encompassed within one person.

## The Four Loves and Every Person

Yet while we emphasize the importance of finding the one, we also must recognize the importance of finding the loves in everyone. Latter-day Saints teach a universal form of Storge, presided over by loving Heavenly Parents. The revealed knowledge of the doctrine of premortality informs us that we worship God as His sons and daughters before we came to earth. It also compels us to acknowledge that each person we meet "is a beloved spirit son or daughter of heavenly parents, and, as such, each has a divine nature and destiny."[117] C. S. Lewis reflected on this in another of his great works, writing, "It is a serious thing to live in a society of possible gods and goddesses, to remember that the dullest most uninteresting person you can talk to may one day be a creature which, if you saw it now, you would be strongly tempted to worship."[118] For Latter-day Saints, this is not just a nice devotional thought, but is also informed by modern revelation. Through the work of Jesus Christ "the worlds are and were created, and the inhabitants thereof are begotten sons and daughters unto God" (D&C 76:24). Reflecting on these staggering truths, Lewis continued, "It is in the light of these overwhelming possibilities, it is with the awe and the circumspection proper to them, that we should conduct all of our dealings with one another, all friendships, all loves, all play, all politics. There are no ordinary people. You have never talked to a mere mortal. Nations, cultures, arts, civilizations—these are mortal, and their life is to ours as the life of a gnat. But it is immortals whom we joke with, work with, marry, snub, and exploit."[119] It is also in the light of these truths we must carefully exercise how to nour-

117 *The Family: A Proclamation to the World*, paragraph 8.

118 C.S. Lewis, *The Weight of Glory*, (New York: HarperOne, 2001), 45-46.

119 Ibid.

ish others through our Eros, Philia, Storge, and most important of all, our Agape.

## The Four Loves and the Source of All Love

Latter-day Saints hold no monopoly on the four loves. They are widespread among all of God's children. But the Saints are set apart as the custodians of a number of special truths that, used properly, can allow the four loves to reach their eternal potential. Over two centuries ago, when God and Jesus Christ appeared to Joseph Smith in the Sacred Grove, they began this Restoration of sacred truths, including their relationship to the four loves. In the most widely used account of the First Vision, the Prophet related that when the Savior spoke, he told him "that all their creeds were an abomination in his sight" (Joseph Smith—History 1:19). This statement has always seemed like a harsh indictment of the state of Christianity at the time of the First Vision. Why did the Savior feel the creeds were "an abomination?" Most Latter-day Saint discourse surrounding this subject focuses on the revelation confirmed to Joseph that the Father and the Son are two separate beings. Just as important, however, is what the creeds of the time said about the nature of God.

One of the most prominent creeds circulating in Joseph Smith's day was the Westminster confession of faith, first composed in 1647. This document was and still is associated with Presbyterianism, the faith Joseph Smith's mother and several family members became associated with. In discussing the nature of deity, the Westminster confession defines God as "a most pure spirit, without body, parts, or passions."[120] The First Vision and subsequent revelations to Joseph Smith restored the truth of God as a being with an exalted physical body, but what about the confession's teaching that God has no passions? Christians, in their attempt to exalt God and Jesus Christ, removed them from the world of mortals entirely, including charging them with a lack of passions—a lack of feeling? In contrast, the revelations of the Restoration depict God and Jesus Christ as driven by passion, by their love for the human family. In the earliest account of the First Vision, recorded by the Prophet in 1832, Joseph recalled that after his experience with

120 *The Westminster Confession of Faith,* 8-9, accessed August 25, 2020, https://www.pcaac.org/wp-content/uploads/2019/11/WCFScriptureProofs.pdf

the Father and the Son, his "soul was filled with love, and for many days I could rejoice with great joy."[121]

It was just as important for Joseph to know the love of the Father and the Son as it was for him to know they are separate beings. God is a being who experiences Eros, Philia, Storge, and Agape. Jesus Christ likewise experiences and exemplifies each of the four loves. In several of the accounts of the First Vision, the first words spoken by the Savior to Joseph were "Thy sins are forgiven thee," an unmistakably manifestation of agape.[122] In a revelation given years later, the Savior told the Saints, "Ye are they whom my Father hath given me; ye are my friends," a sign of the Philia the Savior feels for his disciples (D&C 84:63).[123] In another revelation, the Savior commanded, "thou shalt love thy wife with all they heart, and shalt cleave unto her and none else," showing the importance of pure Eros between those who enter into marriage covenants (D&C 42:22).[124] Finally, the crowning revelations of the Restoration create a chain of divine Storge in which parents and children are connected to each other and to God. Speaking of those who enter into this divine connection, the Savior promised, "Then shall they be Gods, because they have no end; therefore shall they be from everlasting to everlasting, because they continue; then shall they be above all, because all things are subject unto them. Then Shall they be Gods, because they have all power" (D&C 132:20).[125]

Therein lies the great lesson of mortality. We must learn what love is, how it is manifest, and how we nourish it in all of its forms. Not only is knowing love and giving love the key to our happiness and fulfillment here on earth, but it is also the key to what we have the potential to become in the eternities. Learning to love is learning to become like God.

---

121 "History, circa Summer 1832," p. 3, The Joseph Smith Papers, accessed August 25, 2020, https://www.josephsmithpapers.org/paper-summary/history-circa-summer-1832/3

122 «Journal, 1835–1836," p. 24, The Joseph Smith Papers, accessed August 25, 2020, https://www.josephsmithpapers.org/paper-summary/journal-1835-1836/25

123 "Revelation, 22–23 September 1832 [D&C 84]," p. [3], The Joseph Smith Papers, accessed August 25, 2020, https://www.josephsmithpapers.org/paper-summary/revelation-22-23-september-1832-dc-84/3

124 "Revelation Book 1," p. 64, The Joseph Smith Papers, accessed August 25, 2020, https://www.josephsmithpapers.org/paper-summary/revelation-book-1/48

125 "Revelation, 12 July 1843 [D&C 132]," p. [3], The Joseph Smith Papers, accessed August 25, 2020, https://www.josephsmithpapers.org/paper-summary/revelation-12-july-1843-dc-132/3

# Postlude: The Beginning and the End of the Four Loves

There is one last story of the mortal lifetime of Adam, another one of the plain and precious truths taken from the scriptural record and restored in the latter days. Near the end of his life, Adam called together his righteous posterity. His strength waning, he brought them all to the place he made his home with Eve and gave them a final blessing. In return, Adam's children rose up and blessed him. The Savior Himself appeared and blessed Adam (Doctrine and Covenants 107:53-57). Eve is not mentioned in the story, and we may assume that she had passed on when this final blessing took place. Three years later Adam passed into the next life as well. But the important part of the story is that at the end of his life, Adam found himself surrounded by the ones he loved. The love he and Eve shared, the very thing that caused them to leave Eden, had created a new Eden. Their love had grown into multitudes of descendants who gathered to gain a final blessing and in turn honor their parents. It is as important for us to remember this episode in Adam-ondi-Ahman as it is to remember the Fall of Adam and Eve from Eden. A life begun by a cursing in Eden ended with a blessing in Adam-Ondi-Ahman.

The final appearance of Adam and Eve was recorded by the prophet Joseph F. Smith in 1918. President Smith saw a vision of the world of spirits on the day that Jesus Christ died on the cross and arrived there. He described an "innumerable company of the spirits of the just, who had been faithful in the testimony of Jesus while they lived in mortality" (Doctrine and Covenants 138:12). President Smith saw that this "multitude [was] filled with joy and gladness, and were rejoicing together because the day of their deliverance was at hand. They were assembled awaiting the advent of the Son of God into the spirit world, to declare their redemption from the bands of death" (Doctrine and Covenants 138:15-16). At the head of this vast congregation he saw our first parents, still together, still in love, and still with their family. President Smith even noted that Eve was surrounded by "many of her faithful daughters who had lived through the ages and worshiped the true and living God" (Doctrine and Covenants 138:39).

The story of Adam and Eve is still being written, but it is significant to note that in the final glimpse we have of them, they were welcoming their descendant, Jesus Christ, back home with open arms. In a continuing circle of love, Christ blessed Adam and Eve near the end of their mortal journey, and they in turn welcomed him into the world of spirits for a brief stay until His return to earth through His resurrection. While Latter-day Saints often testify that Jesus Christ lives and His story continues, it is also important to note that Adam and Eve also live, and their story continues into the eternities.

The story of Adam and Eve is so rich with meaning that there is little wonder it is the story used in the temple to teach all men and women. Elder Bruce C. Hafen once commented, "We first learn the temple's teachings about marriage in the story of Adam and Eve—the primal story of the temple. A friend once asked me, 'If Christ is at the center of the gospel and the temple, why doesn't the temple endowment teach the story of Christ's life? What's all this about Adam and Eve?'"

Elder Hafen continues, "I have come to feel that the life of Christ is the story of giving the Atonement. The story of Adam and Eve is the story of receiving the Atonement, amid the sometimes-formidable oppositions of mortality."[126]

Through their struggles the first couple came to know every type of love. They knew Eros through their romantic attraction toward each other as they brought children and family into the world. They experienced philia as they labored side by side to provide food and shelter for their growing family. They felt storge for their children as a natural, uplifting, and sometimes heart-wrenching condition of mortality. But the key component to provide their lives with meaning and significance was agape, the pure love of Christ. Elder Hafen explains, "Adam and Eve were the first people to receive the Atonement of Jesus Christ. They were also the first parents to know the love a new child brings, the soul-stretching sacrifices of raising a child, and the agony of watching children use their agency unwisely."[127]

How would we classify the first story of humanity, a story central to our worship in the temple as well as our understanding of the purpose of life? It is ultimately a love story. A story of all of the Four Loves, melded together into the beautiful mortal life of two people who loved each other. Now the seed of their mortal years expands into an eternity. The loves shared by two people become the seed of an entire universe. Like their Heavenly Parents before them, the nourishing power of their love will eventually grow to fill the span of eternity. This divine cycle begins anew with every couple and every person who begins to know the Four Loves.

---

126 "The Temple and the Natural Order of Marriage," *Ensign*, September 2015.

127 Ibid.

# About the Author

Casey Paul Griffiths is a professor of Church History & Doctrine at Brigham Young University in Provo, Utah. He teaches and researches Latter-day Saint history dealing with controversial and lesser-known stories among the Saints. He holds a Master's Degree and PhD in Education from BYU. He has taught at Education Week, Especially for Youth, and the Mormon History Association. He has traveled extensively studying international education and Latter-day material history, working with diverse Restoration movements, including Community of Christ and The House of Aaron. He is the co-author of What You Don't Know About the 100 Most Important Events in Church History along with Susan Easton Black and Mary Jane Woodger. He has also won awards for his work on the international history of the Latter-day Saints, and authored numerous articles, essays, and book chapters on the history of the Saints. He is a member of the Mormon History Association and the John Whitmer Historical Association. A lifelong Latter-day Saint, he has served as a Bishop, teacher, and missionary for the Church. He lives in Saratoga Springs with his wife and four children.